MW01205687

LIFE
A Mysterious Journey

New Age Books

New Delhi (India)

LIFE: A MYSTERIOUS JOURNEY

ISBN: 978-81-7822-489-3

First Indian Edition: 2016

© 2016 by Svāmī Pūrṇā

Published by
NEW AGE BOOKS
A-44, Naraina Industrial Area, Phase-I
New Delhi (India)-110 028
E-mail: nab@newagebooksindia.com
Website: www.newagebooksindia.com

Library of Congress Cataloging-in-Publication Data
Pūrṇā Svāmī
ISBN 978-81-7822-489-3
Includes Foreword, glossary.
Spirituality

Printed and published by
RP Jain for NAB Printing Unit
A-44, Naraina Industrial Area
Phase-I, New Delhi-110 028. India

Foreword

Many readers have already been introduced to the Teachings of Svami Purna (Svamiji), who is a true living Teacher and Master. He teaches following the revered and highly respected oral tradition of discourses. This selection has then been transcribed with dedication. It should be reiterated that when He gives a discourse, Svamiji deals with diverse groups, different nationalities, backgrounds or cultures. He teaches – in a uniquely accessible manner – the profound spiritual tradition that has perennial and universal relevance for all of humanity and remains of paramount importance today. As a true world Teacher, Svamiji's Teachings represent Universal Knowledge and Wisdom that cuts across all barriers in the evolution towards becoming whole.

It is vital to mention that teachers generally fall into one of two categories:

• those who have information, theoretical and book knowledge, who have some achievement in life and recognition in the world through scholarly presence, yet do not practice what they teach; or

• Teachers who have attained great Knowledge and Wisdom – through traditional spiritual training or enlightenment and through the practice and implementation of the Teachings in their lives – and who have lived and continue to live according to the principles that they teach.

Svamiji continues to give – and live – the Teachings in order to inspire those who are prepared to learn and grow as a priority in this life, in the spirit of responsibility for self. As with all of Svamiji's guidance, there is no mistaking the key message that responsibility for self and one's own happiness and development is crucial to a balanced and healthy life and to attain real understanding in the debate over the meaning of life and one's purpose or swadharma.

Life: A Mysterious Journey has particular relevance and application to the individual's current life and practical concerns. This publication explores an approach to living – or way of life – that is reflective of the perennial Wisdom found in the original Vedic and Sanskrit texts that has been tested over many Ages. Indeed, the discourses set out here represent a key source in an individual's search for Universal Truth, joy and fulfillment. In my view, this book reveals the value of a way of life that can be embarked upon whatever one's age, stage in life or background and wherever one lives in this world. It can be read again and again and, with each reading, offers more perception and wisdom.

Dr Linda S Spedding
Vice President, Adhyatmik Foundation, Inc.
London, September 2014

Sri Sri Sri
Svami Purna Maharaj

Svami Purna is a Spiritual Master who holds doctorates in medicine, psychology, philosophy and literature. He has been given the title "Vidya Vacaspati," meaning Lord of Learning and Knowledge. Beyond any particular method or tradition, His Teachings address all aspects of the human condition, encompassing the search and pathway that lead to spiritual understanding and fulfillment. His profound Wisdom provides answers to life's deepest questions and makes the spiritual Path practical, inspirational, and accessible to all who wish to realize their full potential. He teaches the way to lead a healthy, balanced and meaningful life, and, for those who are ready, He shows the way to Liberation in this lifetime. As the late Prime Minister of India, Morarji Desai, who, as a centenarian, led a very balanced and spiritual life under Svamiji's guidance, said, "There are many gurus who have found fame in the West, but Svami Purna is one of the very few who are also greatly revered in India."

Table of Contents

ॐ

1

Life: a Mysterious Journey

We have talked about the fact that life is a continuous journey many times before. Not only is it a journey, but it is also a puzzle, a mystery, a mysterious as well as a mystical experience. When you understand the principle of life, everything will fit into the puzzle. When you are ignorant, you attract suffering, pain and torture. Not only do you attract these negative elements, but you continue to create negativity in the same vein until you feel you are drowning while struggling to keep afloat. Then the whole life feels like a drowning experience. Some of you may have seen someone drowning in a film or you may have had that experience yourself – it is a very painful and frightening experience. You are struggling to live, yet the water seems overwhelming, tossing you up one minute, and pulling you down in the next. You are desperate to cling to something that will help save your life.

When one is ignorant, life can be like a drowning experience, but when one is wise, life becomes a blissful experience full of joy, happiness and contentment. Then the way you see life, the way you comprehend everything, becomes very different. This is reason enough to follow the Path of Knowledge. The Teacher does not have to convince anyone why they should follow the Path of spirituality. It is your choice whether you want the drowning experience or the experience of contentment and fulfillment. It is your decision. The world generally seems to

1

be caught in a drowning experience at the moment. However, it does not have to be like that; there is a choice, there is an alternative. The choice is yours to follow the Path of joy or the path of suffering. So many examples have been given.

For instance, we have explored the example of the bird; the great poet-saint Kabir visualized the life force as a bird. He lived in a rural village where it was his custom to watch the birds as they build their nests, flying out every morning to gather food and returning to the nest at sunset to take care of domestic duties. That is the daily routine, leaving in the morning, flying joyously in the open sky, catching food, and by sunset enjoying the homecoming to the nest. Kabir described the life force as a bird, breathing in and breathing out, and observed that one day, the bird does not return. That is life, for one day the body will no longer be compatible with life and, like the bird looking for a new nest, a new body, a new home needs to be found. It will not be the end of your life, rather there will be continuity.

You say that when people die then the relatives and friends mourn. Consider this: why do they mourn? Why are they sad, unhappy? Have you asked yourself this question? Is it that they miss the comfort of not having this person around any longer? Is it attachment? Is it a question of benefit – positive or negative? Does it affect them financially? Think about this, for essentially all those sentiments are meaningless. The only thing you should consider carefully is whether you have had a joyful, happy and meaningful interaction with others, a time of fulfilling communication. If you have not had a happy time with someone this can be a lesson to you, whereas when you enjoy shared happiness, that in itself produces fulfillment. All other thoughts of sadness and mourning do not derive from the *Atmik* or Knowledge point of view, but merely from the human point of view.

It is like celebrating your birthday with candles and cake – what is the use of that?[1] Actually this should be a time for reviewing your life. Ask yourself: have I used my time well? If not, there is still opportunity to utilize your time. Look at your account: have you defaulted on anything? Have you spent more than your income? Are you going bankrupt? Consider the many countries in the world that have overspent recklessly and are now in financial or economic trouble while still complaining about having to "tighten the belt." The same principle applies to you personally. There is a proverb in India: Stretch your leg only as far as your *chadra* (blanket) goes. If your *chadra* is short, then your feet will be cold. The point is: have you utilized your time and your energy appropriately?

From the human point of view, "death" is a terrible loss because that person is not going to come back in the same body. That is the reason for you to project a sense of love and compassion. Have you brought that love and compassion into the real life? Have you learned from the experience of loss, or do you continue the same negative habits with those still around you? It is so sad when families get together and quarrel, but unfortunately it is quite common. A family may have a reunion for two or three hours and all they do is argue and quarrel – sometimes with resulting enmity that can last for years. The question remains: where is your sense of affection, your sense of love, of compassion, of belonging and of family-ness? If these sentiments are absent, then your relatives or friends are merely *that* – just for names' sake. When reviewing whether you have loved a person enough, the example of Krishna comes to mind,

---

1 See discourse in "Birthdays" *So You Shall Know The Truth*

who left Vrindaban, never to return again. When Krishna's friend Uddhava goes to teach the *gopis* to overcome their suffering of pain and separation, he had to realize that the *gopis* had advanced to a level when each cell of their bodies was filled with Krishna consciousness.[2]

There is no sense of mourning, because the whole idea is to uplift that person to a level where there is only love and bliss. When you have experienced the loss of a loved one, only one question should arise: did I love this person enough? If you have not, it does not mean you should feel guilty or blame yourself; instead it is a time to learn to love those around you. You should radiate love. Learning to communicate love is a big lesson. After all, remember that one day all creatures have to leave their body.

When you are given the parts to a whole in a community wherever you are, whether in the forest or a castle or a palace or near the ocean, it becomes your task to put all the components together, to make them fit – to combine harmoniously what belongs there. This includes happiness, love, dedication, devotion to the Teacher, *seva*/service, affection to each other, help and support. It should be a natural process which is much more enjoyable and meaningful. This does not mean that you make a deal with anyone; you do not get caught into a business-like transaction which can be a very destructive and selfish culture. Love is not a commodity that you trade or transact; affection and feelings are not a business. Sentiments like love and affection are like a fresh mountain spring - a spontaneous feeling of belonging and caring. It is an individual *dharma*. Unfortunately in this day and age, deal making is too common in all relationships.

---

2 See "Uddhava and the *Gopis*" *Stories, Tales and Anecdotes* and "Meditation and *Maya*" *Striving for Wisdom*. Described also in "XXX" *The Truth Will Set You Free*

You have to open your heart and when you open your heart, you cannot make conditions. Unless you open your heart, you cannot obtain or grasp the Knowledge; you cannot perceive the Grace or receive Divine Energy. You have to open your heart and surrender yourself to the Divine. In these circumstances of opening your heart, you do not consider rewards or have expectations. In fact, any kind of expectation is not relevant in a loving relationship: otherwise, sooner or later, it will break down. On one hand, business is business and that has much limitation: buying and receiving, you get something, you give something – that is all. On the other hand, the Path of spirituality, of love and joy, is to open your heart. Kabir again gives the example of living life that is a *living life*, when you open your heart sincerely. In many countries for example, when a woman marries, she is not just marrying the man but rather countless relatives who may make life difficult for her. However, she says to her husband: "If I have your love and loyalty, then all this is worthwhile."

When you are connected to the spiritual Source and the Supreme, to your *Satguru*, then the pain in the world no longer affects you as it would normally do. Then you can go through any suffering and pain, because you know that you are protected, you know that you are inspired. Once you know that, you will have that inner strength; once you are connected with the Source, nothing really matters. Then there are only two things to do: the Ultimate and the immediate. As regards the fulfillment of all your relationships, including your family, mother, father, sister and brother, also consider whether they have been fulfilling relationships or stormy negative battles. Ask yourself how far you have contributed to the negative energy and conduct. Review this objectively and from a spiritual perspective.

From the human point of view, any loss of life of your

relatives or friends is a great loss. From the spiritual point of view, ask yourself: have I learned a lesson? Have I uplifted myself? Unfortunately, many people who are confronted with a difficult situation, like a death, a financial crisis or some health concern, do not feel that strength although they may have been interested in spirituality before. It all depends on how strong you are in a crisis. This is your challenge. Whatever crisis you may have to face, whether death, money or illness, this is the time when your strength is being tested. If your strength is not enough, you have more *sadhana* to go through. Often you have only pretended to be strong. What happened to your *dharma*, your conviction, your belief, your trust? Times of crisis do happen and when they appear and you lose all the trust, faith and belief in your *dharma*, then what is left is hypocrisy rather than real understanding.

Friendship, or companionship, is equally tested in a crisis. How far does your friend, your companion, stand by you in a crisis? These are tests to assess how far you are grounded in your spiritual understanding. When all is smooth all is well, but when a crisis emerges, do you collapse? Let us say you have to go through one year of pain and suffering and you survive with your values intact – that is a good test. But when the time comes to stand and face the situation, will you crumble and collapse? In the case of a loved one who has left the body, the best thing you can do is to send them loving neutral energy, remembering the good times with that person – in all honesty without fooling yourself. Sending loving thoughts will assist in a smooth or less troubled transition for the one who passed, aiding his/her next development. Remember that all the relatives and friends you interact with – whether negatively or positively – are usually repercussions of the past.

Now what do you want to make with your future? Do

you want to continue with that "twisted knot" of *Maya*? Or do you want to come out of this? Remember that you are equally attached in both emotions: extreme hate and extreme love. Hating someone can take that emotion into the future as can be the love for another person. This is the general rule. The question is: are you working on your relationships, are you working them out — or are you caught into the whirlpool of ongoing emotional attachments?

That is an ongoing process in your life. At times, confusion can make things difficult, yet all the Knowledge and practices you acquire will have to be tested. Many may recall the story of the *yogi* who had become attached to a young deer.[3] His attachment had been so great that in his next life he had to take the body of a deer. Although not an ordinary kind of deer, he had to complete that life as a deer. Sometimes, when you look at some animals, like a cat or dog, you get the feeling that they know exactly why they are in that body.

In this cycle of eternity from a spiritual, *Vedantic* point of view, there is no death and there is no birth. A certain timeframe is given to you; what do you do with that time? The ultimate choice is Enlightenment, total freedom. Before that there are so many layers of development. There is a clear Path for what you have to do. If Enlightenment is the ultimate height, there are many steps to climb and sometimes steps can be slippery, requiring extra mindfulness and care.

There is a concept known as Lifetime Enlightenment. It is a good concept, but if you wish to take up this challenge you cannot just stand by without doing something towards that goal. Just chanting a few *mantras* and doing all sorts of meaningless

---

3   See "Indra's Pearls" *The Truth Will Set You Free*

rituals will not lead anywhere. No, the Path to Enlightenment is a real life. You may decide to let go of anger. Does that really mean 'no anger'? Do you examine your anger? Why do you get angry? Once you explore your triggers for anger, then you should work on that. The same applies to jealousy. This again involves issues of competition and comparison. In the spiritual world there is no such thing as competition and comparison. If you continue to compete and compare, you are far from Enlightenment. You are an individual, a whole being. Why do you want to compete? Is it through competition alone that you are motivated? Competition to stand out and excel may be acceptable in the commercial world, but it has no place on the spiritual Path. Instead, motivate yourself to grow without looking left or right. Your only incentive is to work on self-inspiration. You inspire yourself; there is no need to get jealous, backbite and gossip. You need to remind yourself of that.

If you are looking at someone else's life because you want to learn or improve, that is a good thing, but when you backbite and gossip for your own and others' entertainment, you are actually taking a lot of bad *karma* from that person. Kabir says: "Protect those who are critical of you, because they are taking a lot of your bad *karma*." One who is very critical of you is taking your bad *karma*. Any time you focus on anything, you connect yourself with that thing, that person. With this in mind, why not connect yourself with one who can give you higher and positive energy? This is where the concept of meditation is so very helpful, for during mediation you connect with the Higher Being, Higher Source and Energy. Each time you meditate you are connected with that Energy. Irrespective of whether there is higher or lower energy, when you focus on one aspect or person, you are connected. That is how it works.

Consider a violent man who may have abused, attacked or assaulted you and treated you in every negative way. Think of that person: does it give you a good or bad feeling? Of course you feel anger, depression and often you may berate yourself: "How could I have tolerated all this abuse?" Feeling so bad about a memory has instant results, making you utterly miserable. The point is that you are vulnerable to any connection with any energy. But you do have a choice to connect with a Higher Energy. This is why the idea of *satsang*, association with Higher Energy - energy that is higher than you - is so important. You associate with that which is higher. That is the value of *satsang*: growing and developing further.

This whole cycle of life is a beautiful experience. It is also a mystery or mystifying puzzle. To put it all together is your task. You need to work toward Enlightenment – however distant it may seem. Since it is the highest goal, it does not happen just like that. You need to make ongoing effort. You have gone through anger and you know what anger is and you work on dealing with it; you have gone through greed and you know what it is and you deal with it; you have gone through your desire, your lust, your jealousy, your hate – you know all those elements. Now you shift yourself to happiness, to affection, to love, to understanding, delight and to joy. Since you have gone through all those negative elements it does not mean you need to stay and live in this atmosphere. After all, you know that such qualities create problems for you – lots of suffering and pain. It is time to shift into a higher gear that you may not be dragged back to become their victim. You become the Master. This is your technique to live, your "magic" formula to uplift your life. Living by these techniques you can become your own teacher.

In the process of life, time is very important. Remember

the final utterings of a dying King Henry XIII who, having ruled with absolute power for so many years, regretted the time lost that could not be redeemed. Wealth, power, honor, dignity can all be regained, but the one thing that is gone forever – and cannot be regained – is time. Time is the most precious commodity in your life. What have you done – and what are you doing – with your time in your life? Even if you have not utilized it fully, there is still time to learn and to make proper use of your time and not to get stuck. As mentioned before, people often get stuck when there is a crisis in their lives. Often guilt, sorrow and pain will present a hindrance to progressing further. This is very unfortunate since these are the opportunities for learning and growth.

Many examples have been given over the years, yet the biggest problem is forgetfulness – time and again. It is important to remember and to implement the Teachings. Everything can be a joy, whether cooking, driving, gardening, preparing your house for guests – all these activities can bring joy – a bonus of joy and happiness. Remove the term "work" as a stressful or negative activity from your dictionary. Everything can be a pleasure, or *sadhana* in the spiritual tradition and following the concept of *seva*, including what may be considered to be mundane activities such as sweeping the floor. In an Indian *ashram*, it has been common to find that the person who is sweeping will also be reciting a *mantra* as part of this *sadhana*. It is not easy for the modern mind to comprehend this attitude since the concept of *seva* – of selfless service – does not really exist as such in modern culture. *Seva* is actually a token of love, a token of appreciation. If you want to bring out love, just do *seva*. Cultural differences need not come into this; the energy of service through love is universal. If you want to show your appreciation, you do *seva* and *seva* will wipe out your bad *karma* and create good *karma*.

Life has presented you with a great opportunity. Do not miss it, and do not let it pass by. Death is a transition: it is not the end of you, of the soul. It is merely the end of this body, which, when worn out by age or disease, is no longer of value. The most important aspect is the soul, the Eternal Self. The best attribute you can give to that Eternal Self is to give your loving energy – and that you learn through love. Those who are gone are gone. Those who are here, can you not love them? If you feel you have not loved them enough, here is your opportunity to love. It is quite pointless to lament: "Oh, if only I could bring back that person I could love him or her." Even if you were to make contact with a departed soul, what would you gain – and for that matter, what would the departed soul gain? Guilt and attachment should have no place. Indeed, in traditional India the concept is different. If a husband dies, the wife is left alone and a wise person may remind the wife to consider their children as her late husband's beautiful token where she can feel the husband in the children. It would not be considered a loss since he is still part of the children. Therefore there is no conflict within.

Unfortunately many people create their own conflict. It is important that you try to remove that part of you that creates conflict: instead try to manifest Divinity. There is a love-Divine within you, trying to manifest. Do all those things that are necessary for you to do – whatever is demanded of you as a "cosmic warrior." Whatever task you have been given, carry it out as a brave warrior, not as a coward. The world is your battlefield. You have many forces behind you as well as so many weapons. Do not give up the good cause but keep trying. Anything that is so helpful and good, continue and never give up as you experience this mysterious journey of life.

2

The Importance of Humility

There is a time-honored profound *Bhajan* that goes as follows:

> *"Since I had the privilege and opportunity to have come to the feet of the Master, I lost all interest in the world.*
>
> *I no longer enjoy the worldly delights; instead I drink the nectar of His Wisdom.*
>
> *My eyes are no longer interested in the worldly vision; His very aura is like His manifestation.*
>
> *My ear is no longer interested in listening to the world; instead I listen to His nectar-like rain of Knowledge.*
>
> *My tongue is no longer interested in talking about the world: now I want to sing His praise and the glory of His Divinity.*
>
> *My hands are no longer interested in doing worldly work, but only to serve the Master.*
>
> *My feet are no longer interested to walk around in the market place, but to go to the abode of the Master – where He resides.*
>
> *My emotions, senses and my mind are no longer interested in worldly affairs, but only in His Divine Presence and in the reign of His Divine Wisdom.*
>
> *I have no interest in anything but in the Highest Knowledge and the Wisdom spoken by His lotus mouth."*

You may have heard this beautiful *Bhajan* in *Sanskrit* and what the *Bhajan* was explaining is the significance of humility, lack of ego and merger in order to grow spiritually. The *Satguru* referred to does not make you walk; instead He becomes the Path Himself. You are no longer the meditator, you become meditation itself. You are no longer separate from the whole. You merge, totally.

This *Bhajan* holds a very powerful message, even today. Indeed, modern experts have confirmed that humility is associated with the positive traits of modesty, respect and open mindedness that are essential to be able to learn, implement and to grow in understanding.

Recently a person went on a one-hour train journey to see his Teacher. During this journey that person visualized the Teacher sitting in the train. He was unaware of the train moving and what was passing outside; he did not notice who else was sitting in the train. His mind was totally engrossed and absorbed in the visualization of his Teacher: the *Satguru*. That is meditation. People often ask: "What is meditation?" When your mind is fixed on the Highest of High, that is meditation. Krishna reminded Arjuna: "Fix your mind on Me." Thus when you fix your mind in attunement on the Highest, it is then that the Energy will flow, thereby opening the heart *chakra*.

We have previously discussed the opening of the heart. It is then, when you open your heart, that you will also understand the Knowledge. You will grasp the meaning and assimilate it. It will not just be words coming to your ears. The great mystic-saint Tulsidas said: "My ear was like a mouse hole until I heard the Wisdom of the *Satguru*, but now my hearing is attuned to the words and the Wisdom of the *Satguru*."

It is vital to be humble and sincere, to have more humility: only then can you develop Divine Love. A great example is in the *Ramayana* and in the story of Rama and Lakshman. When the demon king Ravana was dying, Rama asked Lakshman to go and learn from Ravana. Lakshman was confused and questioned: "We just fought him and he was our enemy, what can he teach me?" However, Rama insisted that Lakshman must go and learn from Ravana who was also a greatly learned being. Ravana may not have been the final Divinity, but he was certainly an advanced and knowledgeable individual. Rama wanted to teach Lakshman humility. Lakshman had many renowned roles including the following:

- Brother of Rama who was an incarnation of Vishnu; and
- incarnation of the Śeṣanāga, the world snake upon whom Vishnu relaxes with His consort Lakshmi (now Sita).

This meant that he felt himself above the need to learn from a demon king. Therefore humility was an important lesson for him.

The relevance of role-play is also important. Visualize this example of the *lila*: Vishnu relaxing in the vast ocean, lying on the coils of the cosmic snake Śeṣanāga while His consort Lakshmi is massaging His Feet. Who knows, but perhaps because they were a little bored with all the relaxation and, seeking some excitement, they decided to incarnate in the respective human roles. Those who have read the *Ramayana* will appreciate the amount of excitement that this decision engendered. The Divine, Highest of Beings decides to incarnate as Rama, in human form, to experience human emotion, to go through all the process of human life, including being exiled for fourteen years in the forest. According to the plot, Lakshmi, now Sita, born and living in the palace when married to Rama, decides to join her husband in exile, when she is kidnapped by the demon king Ravana. Thus Vishnu became Rama, Lakshmi became Sita and Śeṣanāga the cosmic snake became Lakshman. Such is the greatest *lila*, the greatest Divine Play – based on their own acceptance. Once caught in the human drama, they had to play it out.

The interesting point is that this drama had been written many years previously by Valmiki, a former thief and robber who, after having been initiated by Narada, the Cosmic Sage and Traveler, eventually became a High Being. Valmiki wrote the epic *Ramayana* before Rama actually incarnated. Vishnu could not disappoint His devotee Valmiki – who had laid down all these events long before – and He decided to play out and fulfill His assigned role. Thus the "players" all incarnated and played the story exactly as it had been written.

Shiva, the great Lord of destruction and re-creation who was beyond birth and death, observing this magnificent play, became so fascinated that He also wanted to participate in the great *lila*. He incarnated as the great Hanuman who served Rama. It is interesting how many of the Divinities decided to partake in this Divine Play, adhering to each detail of Valmiki's written epic.

The *Ramayana* is a fascinating example of countless human issues and difficulties and describes how they can be handled and solved. For example, when Rama goes to marry Sita in Mithila, all the beautiful Maithili women who were in love with Rama were seen to be pining. Rama reassured them that in this life He has to follow the human ideal in every detail; He has to follow all the rules and cannot step out of the role He has taken. "However," He proclaims, "In my next incarnation (as Krishna), I will have no rules and you will all be welcome then." Hence all the beautiful Maithili women incarnated as *gopis* during the time of Krishna, whose life depicted a most colorful way of living. This incarnation gives rise to the second major Indian epic, the *Mahabharata*. It depicts a part of Krishna's life where again the story of human emotions and human manifestation takes place and where Krishna imparts the Divine Knowledge and Teachings on the battlefield of Kurukshetra to His disciple Arjuna. The discourse thus given became the Divine Song, the *Bhagavad Gita*. All eighteen chapters of this most profound treatise of philosophy were born on the battlefield. Krishna addresses a despondent Arjuna who does not want to fight: "You think you are the doer? You are not the doer; you just think so. You have been selected for this role."

This is an illustration for everyone to understand that, similarly, individuals are selected to fulfill their role as a mother, father, child, leader, ruler, activist and so on. You have a role which has been assigned to you for your best performance. Are you playing that role fully? The moment you think that you are the doer, you are inviting trouble. Rather think: "I am merely an instrument, things are done through me." If you are not fulfilling your divinely assigned role, someone else will do it and your part will become insignificant and your *karmic* credit will be lost. The point is: just because an individual is not ready, this does not mean the work or play will stop.

The *Satguru* is here to disseminate the Knowledge. Do you want to be a distributor of that Knowledge; do you wish to be a vehicle, an instrument? Can you live in true humility? Then you are welcome. But if you cannot do it, someone else will do it. The Divine Work will not wait for anyone to be ready; it will continue regardless of whether someone is ready or not. Opportunity is given to everyone. The work will continue, the *lila* will go on. This is the mystery of creation. However, for those who are striving, the Divine manifestation will take place.

When Rama incarnated, all the Deities also incarnated. When Krishna incarnated, all Divine Beings incarnated too – some as trees, animals or stones – to participate in the great Cosmic *Lila*. All knew that Krishna would participate and play the great Cosmic Play. None of the Divine Beings wanted to be left out: they took whatever place or part they could find.

A further Divine *Lila* occurred between the Master and His disciple during the time of the Buddha. Ananda was always fearful, insecure and concerned for their safety, wanting to avoid danger. You cannot hide from danger, or you will be hiding forever. You also cannot avoid danger; it is part of life and eventually you have to face it. Ananda represents humanity in its fearfulness, anxiety and stress and the Buddha, the *Satguru*, has to teach, encourage and correct His disciple. The Teacher, the revered Master, becomes weary of this role. Consider the example of a parent, a mother especially, constantly directing and encouraging her child to do what she feels is safe and right. She protects, directs, feeds, cleans and teaches the child. A mother is also a *Guru* – in fact she is your first *Guru* – and her maternal selfless energy continues regardless. A child can be raised with a "spiritual lullaby," the mother repeating: "You are pure, you are complete, you are whole, this world is only a dream, remember that." It is interesting that many mothers do not realize that they are actually the child's first teacher.

Similarly, the disciple and *Guru* relationship is eternal and ongoing. Indeed, in India there was a tradition that parents would offer their child to the *Guru* to learn and grow spiritually. At times however, when a child was conceived by the parents through the Grace of the *Guru*, as the child was born and grew, the parents exhibited some fear that the Master may claim the child to become His disciple. They felt afraid even though the child was conceived through Divine Energy. Their human possessiveness and ego were displayed. However, the essential understanding of this tradition was recognized. The child was to be reared or brought up by the *Satguru* in the spiritual atmosphere with Divine Teachings and fulfill its destiny that one day it may become an Enlightened Soul.

The traditional relationship between *Guru* and disciple is based on Knowledge and fearlessness and focused on liberation. But before the disciple can be liberated, the *Guru* has to impart strength and clarity, overcoming obstacles of the ego. Generally disciples have a lot of doubt, fear and confusion. In some societies people may say that they were confused if they do not wish to understand, whereas others will claim that it was a misunderstanding – although both understood very well. Nevertheless, even if you are confused, confusion is a process you have to go through. By way of example, your weakness may be fear of the dark and your Teacher may ask you to go to a lonely place at night without a light. How would you handle that? The Teacher will make you go through that which you are scared of. If you are scared of water and you do not know how to swim, the first thing the Teacher may do is to throw you into the water. That is one process of learning: shock therapy. Whatever you are afraid of, you have to go through. You have to face and confront your weakness. You have to be strong. One of the conditions of Enlightenment is that you have to be strong: it is not the way of one who is feeble or scared. It is the Path of one who is courageous. It is a mystical journey where you must overcome those things you dislike the most – or those that frighten you the most. All must be approached in the spirit of humility and trust.

You will be put into a difficult situation where you must find a way out. That is *sadhana*; that is *tapasya*. And you will have to go through *sadhana* and *tapasya* to achieve understanding. The mystical Eternal Journey will continue in the circle of life.

By way of example, consider another small circle: the wheel on a car. Such a small wheel can take you to so many places – just by going round and round. Even the wheel of a car is a *chakra* – like the seven energy wheels circulating the energy within your body. When indicating the body, Patanjali refers to the vehicle and Kabir refers to the palace – in that great vehicle the Lord, your Beloved, is dwelling and residing. Your body is both the palace and the vehicle to take you to your destination.

What is represented by each *chakra* in your body? It is like a *mandala*, a big circle. Life is like a circle and the *mandala* is the mystery of the *chakra*, the great circle. The world is also a circle – just look at the cycle of life – it is a circle from birth to childhood, to adulthood, to aging and final disintegration, what is usually termed "death." You may go travelling all over the world, and then you return, completing the circle. *Vedic* tradition calls this "a never-ending circle." Other ideologies describe places like heaven and hell, and, although no one really can tell you what happens there, the imaginary tales are vast and vivid. The concept of *karma* and responsibility for Self – the positive learning potential – unfortunately is missing from this approach.

Vedic philosophers were very wise when they said: "Let them go in circles and let them work out the mystery." While you are going round in circles, try to understand the meaning. That is your human challenge; that is your task to determine how to get out of this apparently never ending circle. Consider nature – it is also an ongoing circle of seasons – spring, summer, autumn and winter – repeating itself year after year. Clouds, rain flowing back into the river, sun, clouds, and rain again – that is the *mandala*.

In the circle or play of life, you can be the smallest of the small as well as the mightiest of might. It is in your hands. It is up to you whether you want to be a supreme commander of the universe or a helpless little creature. Even the difference between a prominent scholar and the average person is nil or minute in the great scheme of things – all have the same senses, organs and bodily functions – the only difference is that some have expanded their capabilities whereas others have not. For instance, you can be a frog in the well or a frog of the ocean. There is a story that one frog came from the ocean and accidentally fell into a well where it met the well-frog. The ocean frog said to the well frog: "My friend, this is such a small place. Where I come from the waters are vast." The well-frog did not believe him and replied: "You are a liar, you just want to deceive me. There is not even such a thing as an ocean. This well is all there is." This frog was born in the well, had never been anywhere else and was prepared to die in the well; how could he understand the concept of an ocean? At times, when a spiritual Teacher talks to people in the world, some will say: "What is he talking about?" It is beyond their understanding that the Teacher can show them how to come out of their well and into the ocean.

Mind is so conditioned: it conditions, then it decides and eventually it believes. The power of the mind is so strong that if you tell yourself that nobody likes you – repeatedly – and you go out into the street, everyone may appear hostile to you. If you keep telling yourself that you are no good, you will not even be able to talk properly when you interact with others. If you repeatedly tell yourself that you are bad, naturally you will go about doing nasty things. If you are convinced that nobody is your friend, nobody will be your friend – you will be all alone. However, you have the choice to think that the whole world is your friend. You go about wearing a smile on your face and people will smile at you – maybe not all, but many will smile back. This is the power of the mind. You program yourself, and your programming becomes so ingrained that your body and your senses will start acting accordingly.

There is a very popular substance called *parasmani* in India: anyone who has this substance can touch iron and transform it into gold. The *Satguru* is considered *parasmani* and you are iron, and He can turn you into gold. This is the Eternal Mystical Journey, a fulfilling and happy journey. You have every reason to be happy and to invite your mind to join you. If you want to be happy and another person is not, what can you do? The smaller pot can fit into the bigger pot, not the other way around. So if you are a happy person you cannot join the other person in unhappiness. The answer is to maintain your happiness and hope that one day that person will start associating with your happiness. Keep trying, that is your *karma*, that is your work, and that is the answer to your question. You need to fulfill your role to keep playing your tune of happiness, of positivity, of hope and of freedom. Eventually others will hear and will join.

In the meantime, you live here on Earth and you have tasks to fulfill, both physical and spiritual. Come down to Earth and develop love; this is something tangible. It is something you can feel, you can give and you can receive. Since love is connected with bliss, it is connected with all that lies further and beyond. Catch this substance – which is within your grasp – with humility. For the time being, forget all that is not within your reach. Bliss is within your heart to experience: knowing, growing, bringing fulfillment to your physical body, your emotional aspect and the deepening of your soul. That will eventually bring Enlightenment. You can liken this to lightning, which takes just a fraction of a second and the whole Earth landscape within your visual field is brightly illuminated. Consider this a "lightening" in your brain and in your heart.

Start with love and believe it, feel it in every day – with sincerity and humility – and remind yourself as a practice:

- I will not allow myself to get angry, frustrated, depressed and insecure and fearful.

- I will allow myself to feel happy, confident and look to a beautiful future.

- I will feel positive with love in my heart and give as much as I can to others, even though they may not appreciate or value this (which does not matter).

- I will be like the sunshine.

- I will radiate fragrance like flowers; and

- I will take responsibility to make myself happy and my happiness will benefit all those who come into my contact spreading this positive energy. If not today or tomorrow, some day they will feel my vibration and my happiness.

Repeat this *mantra* as a practice every day and remember the Teaching with humility; then you will see the difference in your life.

3

Spirituality has no Phases

There are many phases in one's life. Indeed, when we talk about phases in one's life, we have to examine this statement carefully as, biologically speaking, there are also phases your body goes through. From birth to age five is your babyhood, after that from age five to ten is your second phase of childhood. Each biological phase will have a different manifestation. Adolescence is the third phase from age ten to eighteen, followed by young adulthood from age eighteen to thirty; then thirty to forty, forty to fifty; fifty to sixty; sixty to eighty and so on. These are the biological phases. During each of these biological phases you will manifest differently. As a baby you get to know life by learning through playing, eating, sleeping. These three activities are the major components in the baby's life. As you get older, although your manifestation will vary, these three aspects will remain. The mindset of age five to ten will be different: it is a very important time where valuable lessons can be incorporated in the child's life through playful learning. For instance, if the teacher is creative he or she can use the sounds of selected animals as a playful, yet creative, way of teaching. This can contribute richly to the child's concept of the world. It is the age when many impressions are created.

Moving from age ten to eighteen can often be regarded as a potentially dangerous age, when the emerging hormones can lead to recklessness at times. Because of hormonal interplay, there is also rapid physical and biological development and the results can be very mixed. There can be extremes of emotions of all kinds. It is also the age when, in school, you think you know it all and have an answer for everything. Such is the nature of biological development; you feel you have endless physical and emotional strength. After the age of eighteen the feeling is that you have all the time in the world because you have great physical strength and imagination. Although there is much turmoil and psychological upheaval, you may feel invincible. In modern day society – especially post World War II – it has become difficult for parents to manage their teenagers, particularly following the development of information technology. Interestingly, this phenomenon is rather less pronounced in places remote from modern culture. Maybe the modern post-war culture of processed food and isolationist society is to blame. It is also a climate which can engender much negativity. Adolescence is an age when you are not in control of your emotions and you can become victim of your own emotion and mind, as you have not yet reached emotional maturity. You have passion without experience. It is interesting to see the manifestation of someone who married at age eighteen and later felt that they had missed out a great deal in life. It is a fact that in different biological phases of life, different emotions and behavior manifest.

There was a time when teenagers had a certain ideology and ideals. They were moved by the vision of a better world, better environment, improved family and community, often with some spiritual and humanitarian aspiration and higher values. It seems that nowadays these qualities have disappeared and been replaced by modern and material desires.

It is not my purpose to outline the different manifestations of each biological age. That information you can easily find in psychology and biology books. I am merely trying to portray the recent changes that have become so dominant in the world. On the other hand, someone who has been engaged in spiritual practices for ten or more years and then deviates from such practices or stops altogether and considers it a "phase" has to understand that in true spiritual pursuit there are no phases at all – rather there are stages of development.

The issue of phasing is strictly on the physical level, definitely not on the spiritual level. Of course there are times when your progress may appear to be slow, that is possible. But there is no such thing as stating that this is my phase of non-practice and non-belief. You may be able to change various physical components of your body nowadays, but you cannot change your soul; it is the only one you have. Even in your next incarnation, it will still be the same soul and it will continue to carry all you have done, spoken and thought. Attributing a phase to your soul is not possible; you cannot say that: "I had ten years of a spiritual phase – or a phase of chanting *mantra*, or meditation, or studying spiritual texts – and now I am having a material phase." If this is your thought, you have not understood what spirituality is. There is no substitute, nor replacement for spirituality – and there is no phasing-out.

Then what happens if you feel you are phasing-out? Maybe you only thought that you were spiritual or you put on a garment of spirituality, adorning yourself with symbols like *malas*, garlands, orange clothing and similar items? Although some symbols may help with focus and concentration, they do not make you spiritual. Spirituality, the focus on Divinity, is an act of the heart and that heart is connected with your soul. It is not connected with emotion, for emotion is fickle and wavers all the time, like the waves on the water when the wind springs up. Those waves will settle when all is calm again. However, the heart which is connected with your soul is your eternal heart, your Eternal Soul.

You can say that deep down the desire is there. Everyone has desires, many of them physical, emotional, sensual – and then some have spiritual desire. As an individual you are caught into the physical level of consciousness, caught in multiple desires which run you like a program – like a mad dog looking for the fulfillment of its desire. When you have exhausted all the meaningless things of the world, you may one day discover the manifestation and the power of spirituality. Then you are attracted, not because of the spiritual energy, but because of desire energy – thinking that being spiritual, or pretending to be, your desire will be fulfilled. In the madness of desire you may feel that this is the key to having your desire fulfilled. Then you do not mind pretending to be spiritual: however, this is not real.

Spirituality is not some kind of superstition, such as those that deal with mediums or ghosts. The term "spirituality" has been misused, misunderstood or confused with "spiritualism" in the modern culture and often been defamed and denigrated. For example, calling the head of a terrorist organization a "spiritual leader" just because there are people following him is an insult to the meaning of "spiritual." Small wonder that many do not want to be associated with this kind of "spirituality" and with this kind of energy. Many times it is the media who creates these catchy – but misleading – terms.

Let us talk about the real spirituality, the true perennial Knowledge. It is the constant and lasting Knowledge, the internal Knowledge which is eternal. It is the Knowledge of Eternity, which can liberate you in the truest sense, bringing liberation of your heart and your mind, and freeing your soul from the bondage of all *karma*, all desires and all obstacles and ignorance. That Knowledge is the spirituality which frees you from everything – from all pain and suffering completely. It takes you from total darkness to complete Light, to total bliss. This is the ultimate goal and achievement which cannot change. It will always be there until you have reached the final destination. Having reached that goal, you will be in complete control of yourself.

That understanding is not changeable and there is no substitute for it. There is no replacement – just as there is no replacement for the *Satguru*. In the world you can change your ordinary teacher, for instance if you are not happy with their teaching in language or mathematics, you can always find another one. But a true *Satguru* cannot be replaced; how can you even talk about "replacing" a Divine Being? This is utter foolishness. You also cannot replace your soul. It is what it is. You cannot say: "I do not like my soul and therefore I will get another soul." Soul is always pure. Soul is always the Shining Self, the *Atma*, the ever Shining Sun and Light. It is said that the biggest punishment for a human being is to be placed completely isolated in a dark and dingy place with no light whatsoever. Even in such an environment, light is the symbol of bliss. *Vedanta* says: "Those who do not search for light condemn themselves to the darkness of a dungeon."

We are talking of that soul, that Self, that *Atma* which is everlasting, ever new, ever blissful, peaceful and without any kind of flaw. The thought can arise: "How come my soul is so beautiful and I am so miserable?" Aspire to cast away your misery and reach that beauty. As the *Vedas* proclaim: "The Truth is the ultimate good and beauty – *Satyam Sivam Sundaram*." That is your aspiration; that is your beauty, your soul, your Self. All other paths are merely those where the blind lead the blind. Imagine a *Guru* who is blind and a disciple who is deaf. It does not take much imagination to visualize the outcome.

When you begin on your Path you have to be very definite about what you want. You need to decide whether you want to be in the land of desire or you want to go through desire and beyond desire. Do you want to set your goal high or do you want to remain in the mud of desire? You have to be sure and clear about what you are asking. By way of example, someone goes to an embassy and states: "I am requesting asylum" – in other words: "I want protection." However, "asylum" can also mean something quite different and that person might find himself in a mental asylum. The point is you need to be quite definite in setting the right intention or *sankalpa*, stating what you want before you ask. Consider the man who asked his *Guru* that he should always be able to fulfill his desire to count money (meaning for himself). He ended up as a cashier. *Maya*, the great illusion, can fool you and you may get something quite different than what you have asked for. You have a strong desire and want *that* to happen and sometimes you think you want to follow the spiritual Path – after all, you do have the spark of Divinity – but often the worldly desire dominates. Pretension of following the spiritual Path is not uncommon, but should be recognized. It is the nature of desire that it can never be fulfilled. You can go through desire, you can experience desire; however, there can never be fulfillment through desire. It is only fuelling the fire.

How can you explain, when someone pretends to follow the Path and proclaims that he or she wants to serve the Master or Teacher – or humanity or country – and when they encounter some financial distraction the Path is no longer the priority. How do you explain that? It is obvious that the money was in the forefront of their mind. If money is your primary focus, that is certainly not a sign of Enlightenment; it shows clearly where the center of attention is. Even if not verbalized, it explains your inner desire – and your Path has been placed on the back burner. The true Path can never be put on the back burner; it is the very soul of your being. You have to admit that you are in the land of desire, the land of *Maya*. If you claim differently, you will be proven wrong by the very forces of *Maya*. Therefore, it may be safer and more prudent not to proclaim, for whenever you do, you will be caught in the net of *Maya's* manifestation and proven wrong. Similarly, milk, when heated and close to the boil, will appear puffed-up and of much larger quantity. But this appearance is deceptive, for when the heat goes down, the real amount will be obvious. It is very interesting to see the play of *Maya* and how it manifests. I see it all the time how people pretend and how they can fool themselves – not realizing what they want and what they are looking for.

One thing is very clear: on the Path there is no phase, no up and no down; the Path is steady – steady until you reach the summit. Be very clear about this. The Path is always steady, all else is a fluctuation of your desire. You cannot say: "Today I feel spiritual, tomorrow I do not." You are mixing up your goal with your desires, not dealing with the spiritual force or energy. When you do not feel spiritual, that only means that you are not connected, and each time that you are disconnected, this feeling will prevail. Each time you connect, you will feel wholeness. There are no phases on the spiritual Path, only in desire. Phases apply elsewhere, such as physical phases, whether biological, emotional, physical or financial. As I mentioned, in the perennial spiritual realm, there is no such thing as a phase. What I am trying to explain is the need to see yourself where you are; it is like being your own teacher, within your own limited capacity. When you can see where you are, you can walk to your destination. Wherever you are – like when in a big city – you have to establish your exact location so that you may find your way to your destination. Do you want to go straight or take a detour? Unfortunately many people are confused and do not know where they are, whether they are coming or going, so how can they know their destination?

We spoke earlier about the baby, living in three phases of its life, playing, eating and sleeping. The baby is innocent and has no idea about tricks, manipulation or deceit in any form – although it may have learned that crying will bring attention – unlike adults who often have learned many tricks. Indeed, attention seeking is another play of the mind and many tricks are tried even on the Teacher, not realizing that there is no trick the Teacher is not aware of. The irony of the mind is that it thinks it can deceive the Teacher. It is important to look at yourself and your own manifestation fully. In order to have a complete picture or understanding of yourself, you should forget about judgment – about wrong or right – for when you think about wrong or right, you activate your defense mechanism. You do not want to be wrong and therefore defend your act, and when you are right, you expect praise. Rather, see where you are coming from. It is not so much what you do and how you manifest but rather the motivation of your act, speech or thought, as well as the perception of what you are engaged in.

One interesting aspect in your own life is that you do not mind repeating that which has given you pleasure before, whereas you are often reluctant to repeat those things that would help you to advance spiritually in the pursuit of Knowledge. That also gives you an idea of what stage you have reached and where you are by reviewing whether you generally behave negatively or positively. It should be understood that when there is enjoyment of negative activities, this will bring more negativity into your life. For instance, if you live with polluted air or water, your physical symptoms cannot be positive, whereas living in pure air with fresh pure water can benefit you physically. It should be very clear where your interest lies.

The question is why does one enjoy negativity, even in food, company or in entertainment. The fruit of both negativity and positivity is so obvious, yet the tendency to choose the negative seems to prevail, just as the natural tendency of water is to flow down. That is the human dilemma – and the world generally often appears caught into that negativity. Realizing the outcome of negative choices and still making the wrong choice is the biggest trick of *Maya*. On the other hand, when the heart and mind are clear, then you can see everything clearly, as in clear water, and then you can discern how to be in the world but not of the world. That does not mean that you hate anything, for that will only create more hateful reaction. It is more a matter of protecting yourself and your own treasure and understanding. You take care of your own gift of understanding, with the ability to discriminate. As you are walking on the Path, you acquire self-discipline and self-discrimination. This will help you and others when defining your own goal and your Path.

There are countless examples of how people are caught in this game of *Maya* in daily life and what they see is not necessarily what is real. Suffering is created in your mind. For example, when you feel that someone is talking about you, you react – either negatively or positively. It also means that you are empowering that person by letting their action affect you. Why is it not possible to create your own momentum of happiness?

Why should your happiness depend on some other person's behavior? As long as your happiness is affected by the actions of others, you will always be drowning in the seas of happiness and unhappiness. That is something which has to be learned: to acquire your own Knowledge and confidence, thereby building your own foundation that you are connected with the whole. Otherwise there is an ongoing syndrome of sink and swim.

Enough Teaching has been given for you to understand your true being. There is so much Teaching that at times it can appear to be overwhelming. The key is to accept what your mind can cope with. When you can keep your mind calm, peaceful and strong, this will also enable you to become more focused on your goal. The physical reality and the spiritual reality have to be integrated. Once that integration is achieved, you will realize that you are following the comprehensive Path. This is the way to have a dialogue with the Divine and whether you tune into it is your choice. This will require *sadhana*, *tapasya* and practice. The true Search is important, seeking the very life of your existence in contrast to the other ways that can consist of destruction, ignorance and darkness. That is the continuity of your Path, an unbroken journey that has no phases. It is your opportunity to be grounded in your mind and in your emotions, rather than being tossed in the air like a leaf in the wind.

4

Paths of Love

The Path of spiritual progress you have taken can commence as a collective as well as an individual Path. It is collective in the sense of working and celebrating it within a group, being inspired by the collective vibration. However, the more you progress and advance on the spiritual journey, it becomes a very personal or individual Path. While you may be getting support from similarly minded people or from your family – and as long as you can offer them something they like and agree with – it becomes a collective Path.

For a deeper and more meaningful growth you have to take an individual Path, while you may still enjoy some collective interaction. For example: you may wake up in the middle of the night, when everybody is sleeping, and the question comes to mind: "Who am I, what am I doing here, how did I come to this point?" Questions such as these are your own very personal questions. Waking up your family or your companion to question them about your concerns will generally result in an admonishment for you to be quiet and go back to sleep. They may also question your sanity, or at least tell you to defer your "crazy" questions till the morning. Of course, in the morning they may tell you to look at your passport and that will tell you who you are. Promptings like these indicate that you are no longer on the collective path but have taken steps on your individual Path – a very personal, solitary, individual Path.

Indeed, people also have a tendency even to reflect upon the Teacher things that they like, that are meaningful to them; for instance people will offer the kind of food or drink that they like rather than ask: "What would you like, *Guruji*?" The human reflection, even in the intensity of devotion, dedication and love, is based on human conditioning. Yet they all create energy and the extent of purity should be recognized. As an individual, one must make proper inquiry. Similarly, when you take the road of spiritual celebration with a companion, how far do you think your companion will go with you? This is often the stage when you walk alone, as your partner may have their own limitations.

This happened to Mira, the 16th century Rajput princess, daughter of King Ratan Singh, a happy child who, as custom demanded, was married at a very early age. She soon discovered that this marriage did not give her answers to the questions that had been troubling her. One day she made a statement to her husband: "You are the master of my body and my mind, but the master of my soul is Krishna." Naturally her husband was confused; this was something he could not understand. However, he put it aside as a young girl's fantasy, regarding it as just a phase, which, hopefully, would pass eventually.

Instead, it happened that during a court function, Mira, circulating among the guests, began asking people whether they had seen Krishna. People were perplexed and just a little concerned about such a question coming from a princess: how could anyone *see* Krishna? After all, He is just a character in the scriptures, and characters do not step out of books and stories. Krishna remains in the *Bhagavatam* – as Rama remains in the *Ramayana*. How can anyone be expected to see such Divine characters?

In various parts of the world, generations of people do perform various rituals and ceremonies, bowing down and praying to their gods, yet very few will probe *why* they are doing this. Often it has been a family tradition and as such it is just being continued; after all, that is the way it has always been done – and so it will continue, like a time-honored tradition. However, questioning and doubting the rationale, asking if you have seen Krishna, at best you will be considered a "misfit" or even labeled as deranged. After all, during a social function, a party, you do not ask such serious, spiritual questions; party-time is regarded as being for light interaction and not for meaningful discussion.

Mira is looking for Krishna, asking: "Where is Krishna? Have you seen Krishna?" Questions such as these make people uncomfortable and can spoil the light atmosphere. Consequently, Mira is banned from future family gatherings. Of course this makes her very happy, and in her solitude she sings: "The only truth I know is Gopala, Krishna." This very statement indicates her advanced level of consciousness. It also does not mean that she rejects the world, but she is sliding into a different level of consciousness; she is moving into her own individual level of consciousness by the nature of her own understanding. The world she lives in can no longer offer her anything further. She enters into a different world where she dances and sings in Krishna Consciousness. In fact, her banishment from society provides the happy opportunity of solitude she craves where she can sing and dance for her Krishna. Meanwhile her family regards her as crazy and her mother-in-law accuses her of having ruined the family.

Although she is not harming anyone, Mira's very conduct

is like a challenge to the entire family and to the community. She is not behaving in the accepted way, which is to go to the temple, do *puja*, make an offering to God and then come home and look after your husband and family. She is not following the traditional way but has become radical in her behavior – and when your behavior is radical, society labels you as a misfit. In this case, she is a spiritual radical, not following the norm, not behaving in an accepted way. While she is not harming anyone, she has become a social outcast.

Expressing individual freedom is often not acceptable if it is not within the parameters of the prevailing norms: you have to follow society's etiquette. In short, Mira thoroughly upset the status quo of society at that time – five hundred years ago. She became a problem, dancing, singing, even talking to the servants – behavior inconsistent with her social position. Eventually the family decided that something had to be done and the only conceivable way was to remove her permanently. Poison was sent to her, mockingly called "*Prasad* of Krishna." Mira was delighted to receive this gift and drank the poison, yet she survived.

It was decided to hold a family meeting. All the key family members gathered and Mira was called in to "explain" her behavior. Her response was: "Krishna is the only One I know and recognize." Everyone was stunned and horrified, yet still there seemed no way of getting rid of this troublesome woman. She was a liability: a princess who would go into the street, sing and dance with the visiting *sadhus* and ascetics in ecstasy was a huge scandal. Happily for everyone, one day Mira decided to go to Vrindavan – much to the relief of her family, to live in her Krishna Consciousness.

Mira's whole behavior at that time was extremely

courageous, singing and dancing, creating her own inspiring songs and poems with her small *ektara*. It happened that at that time, there lived a renowned spiritual leader in Vrindavan called Jiva Goswami. Mira wanted to see this great and famous Master; however Jiva Goswamiji's life-long vow was to never see a woman. A message was sent to Mira to that effect. Mira's response though was that she thought there was only one Man in Vrindavan and that was Krishna. Who could possibly be the second man? When Jiva Goswami heard this response, he realized that this was no ordinary woman. He agreed to meet her to the astonishment of his disciples. Of course, this news also reached her former family who were just as shocked.

The point is that the intensity of Divine Love is something very different from the normal – give and take of – human love and also from so-called "blind love." If someone were to be asked what they mean by saying "I love you," that person may become upset or angry. People do not like to be pinned down for an explanation of such a statement. Blind love is exactly that – it does not see anything: it also does not see the object of its love clearly – and it does not consider potential consequences. It is intense, blind love, which may last a couple of weeks or months or years, and it does not see the pitfalls of its passion. The temporary intensity of emotion causes the blindness. The interesting part is that the source is actually Divine Love. It is ignorance and motivation – whether known or not – that create a block, and limited – sometimes dangerous – blind love without rules or reason. Then, when the "fever" of love is over and reality strikes, the cost of the experience has to be assessed. You have to reconcile and consolidate. It is very interesting that when you experience that kind of intensity of love, it is just like awakening from a beautiful dream. You want to bring that beautiful dream back, but you cannot. It is accurate to call it "blind love" because you do not know where you are going; you are so blinded that you have no concept of the consequences.

Conversely, if the blind love is Divine Love and part of your individual spiritual Search, the result will be entirely different. For if you love your God or your *Satguru*, it has to be that kind of blind love that requires pure devotion and not anything else. While the ordinary kind of blind love will lead you to chaos, this kind of blind love will lead you to the Eternal Light. That is the difference between the worldly blind love and the Divine blind love. Indeed, in Mira's quest for love, her love is blind and not only is she totally unaware of any consequences, she is not the least interested in what might befall her. Her quest is a total blind love and she does not care about the opinions of others – which is often the human challenge. Essentially, while therefore there is human blind love and Divine blind love, there can be a connection. It is that Divine blind love which makes you immortal. Interestingly, this principle can either transform your life and your energy or lead to stagnation through involvement with mundane or sensual pleasures.

It was mentioned before that you can have a collective celebration with each other – or you can walk the individual Path. A child, left to its own devices, will actually create its own play although, if a companion is provided, the child will also happily play with the companion. But, if just left alone, it has the capability to create a wonderful play for itself with nothing but his hands and maybe some very simple items; a stone, a leaf, a cork, a chair, a blanket, all can become magical tools for the child's play. This ability to create and enjoy its creation is remarkable. Similarly, when you become evolved, you have a tremendous ability to slide into a state of love and pleasure; you bring that reality to yourself. You may no longer depend on inspiration from books or music, any companion or outer stimuli. You will have the ability to arrest that moment, to bring it to yourself and to be content in the blissful state of consciousness.

Such was the state of Mirabai, and mystics like Kabir and Guru Nanak and many other Great Masters throughout history. It was the intensity of their love and devotion that brought them to this blissful state through Divine Love, rather than traditional inspiration or education. Love is very important and when coupled with Knowledge can lead to a blissful state of consciousness, when you can feel and experience Divine Love – bright like the clear moon caressed by a soft breeze, a Divine manifestation of Cosmic Energy. To achieve this state, you have to keep striving individually: and it cannot be achieved collectively.

5

Emotions are like Clouds

Clouds are like your emotions, changing shape and consistency constantly – thicker, thinner, slower, faster—forming and dissolving all the time. Most of you have come across one or several people diagnosed with Bipolar Disorder, a mood disorder based on chemical imbalance in the body. The name explains it well: these people experience both poles of mood extremes from a state of mania to deepest depression. From that vantage point, they are controlled by their emotions as evidenced in the way they feel and act. Unfortunately they totally lose their grounding reality; they are convinced that everything they are doing is right, and their opinion is also right. They have also convinced themselves that everybody else is wrong, including the Teacher. Then the question arises: who is controlling whom? The concept of needing control seems to be a very basic one – even the baby likes to control. That instinct to control also goes right to the top of a nation where just a few individuals like to control the entire country. Many well-known leaders have suffered from bipolar disorder.

The more balanced person is able to regulate their emotions and detach when and where necessary. Moreover, Krishna says that while there are all types of interaction occurring among people, a wise one does not get involved and maintains detachment. Once you get involved, you may be liable to the consequences of the prevailing energy. Therefore non-involvement is the better approach. Non-involvement is the typical quality of an evolved or evolving individual and is a helpful practice.

From the point of the cosmic play, that play, the *lila*, just goes on. Do you get involved in the game of *lila*? If you are an actor and you go on the stage, play-acting is your involvement. However, when going off the stage, that play is over and you are no longer involved. Everyone has a part in the cosmic *Lila* – which is as old as creation. Some people may question: "What is the point of creation at all?" The *jiva* – the individual soul – has to do *something*. Basically, a human being only generally knows how to be active or to sleep; anything else, like meditation or sitting in silence, requires effort. Quietness means "go to sleep" when not quiet it means you need to do something, such as eating and drinking. When you have a guest you feel you have to do something or say something, and often the conversation is about the weather or others. That is how you start communication with a stranger. It seems that activity is related to all creatures, even plant life – all seem to be doing something and interacting throughout the world. Action seems to be a predominant quality of every creature. It is the result of cause and effect. For instance, you react when something happens, but if you do not react that can also cause trouble. By way of example, if you do not speak, your companion may ask: "Why don't you say something? Why are you so quiet, are you feeling alright?" Sometimes one would like to respond: "Yes, I am feeling alright, why don't *you* talk?"

Another example is when asked how you are; it is not enough for an effective communication in the usual life to say "I am fine." People prefer a narration. It is an active world and this world is ruled by emotion; it goes on and on, like the cloud which forms and dissolves. In a way you could consider it resembling a battle of clouds. What you really need is sunshine, for when there is sunshine, the clouds disappear. A rising sun is a symbol of a beginning, a new day. The darkness disappears, and instead there is light, clarity and happiness. The symbol of sunshine can mean anything; it may be a person or an object or Knowledge or a thought; it can even be yourself, depending on what your mind is focused on. There is a common saying, describing someone's depressed mood as "being under a dark cloud."

People who are considered bipolar do not think that they are unhappy because they have accepted that they are right and everyone else is wrong. When depression manifests, it is perceived as a very heavy cloud hanging above them, regardless whether this is due to a thought, a problem or a change in body chemistry. It is interesting that a thought can actually change your body chemistry. Body chemistry is changing all the time, renewing itself constantly. You may want to think about that mystery – and the miracle – of constantly changing body chemistry. You may not realize this, but miracles are happening all the time, be they on a physical, mental, psychological or spiritual level. Unfortunately, people with mental aberration often seem to have an answer for everything, although this is merely a way of satisfying their own ego. That is yet another mystery of the constantly changing and transforming chemistry in the body.

There are different kinds of worlds; for instance, you have an interactive world and a silent world. Yet even in the silent world there is also communication, albeit a different kind of communication. Beyond those worlds there is still much more and at times this can be overwhelming. That is why choosing the Path of *bhakti*, of selfless devotion, is less overwhelming, by bringing a transformation through love for the devotee. Some seekers are more suited to the Path of Knowledge, whereas for one who is very active, *karma* yoga – the *yoga* of dedicated action – may be the fulfilling Path. It is interesting how the philosophy has developed the division: *arth*, resources, *dharma*, implying duty or responsibility as well as your own inner search and conviction, followed by *kama*, the fulfillment of all your desires, and finally *moksha*, liberation.

Quite often the question arises: "What shall I do?" Well, there are plenty of things to do and if you are truly interested you can make a long list of what you can do. Therefore a question of what to do is really a confused question because there is so much to do, that this lifetime is not enough. If you really need to have it pointed out to you, the Teacher will give you a list – a very long list.

Of course the Teacher does not expect you to carry more than you are capable of and knows exactly your capacity and ability. Sometimes a student may ask the Teacher: "What is the mission?" The best reply a Teacher can give is that the mission depends on what the students are capable of. Are they capable of transforming the world? Then that is the mission. Are they capable of disseminating perennial knowledge? Then that is the mission. Therefore, the mission depends on people's individual capabilities, qualifications and willingness; that is how the mission is defined – as it is normally formed by the potential of the individual.

You may have heard the famous quotation by the 16th century poet-saint Kabir: "Those who want to follow me have to burn their houses first." Of course this is not a challenge to commit arson, but a symbolic statement focused on renouncing your attachments to worldly goods and pleasures. You have created and enjoyed your world, you have lived with it, and the time will come when you need to let go. Letting go is very difficult, but in any case, whatever is given to you, it will be taken away from you. The only thing you can do is to make good use of your resources, material and otherwise. All earthly goods will be gone, all relatives and friends will be gone, your physical beauty and strength will be gone, and finally the body will disintegrate or just be a small pile of ashes. Only the *jiva*, the soul, will remain and travel with *dharma's* good deeds. This body, although a marvelous and intricate piece of machinery, is also very fragile, vulnerable and insubstantial. It too will perish. When you consider that some religions depict hell with flames devouring the human, it makes little sense. You know that the human body cannot withstand anything remotely resembling so-called "fires of hell." It was the realization of this very insubstantial aspect of the body – a body that can be consumed by disease and old age – that effected the transformation in Prince Siddhartha, resulting in His total dispassion and disillusionment with the world. He renounced all worldly things and passing pleasures. This complete change of insight eventually led to His becoming the Buddha, the Enlightened One.

What is it that one is so proud of? It is only the boasting energy of the ego. Otherwise usually ego has no function. You can say: "I am this or that or the other." So what? What does it matter? On the other hand, if ego gives you the boost to do something unusual or positive, then ego may have a place in your life."

You may know the example of Tulsidas, a young married man, very much in love with his wife who was briefly away visiting her parents. His longing for his wife was so strong that even during the monsoon time, when the river was too swollen to cross, He managed to cross it with the help of a floating corpse, and with the assistance of a snake he climbed to the window of his in-law's house. When finally, in the middle of the night, he encountered his wife, instead of greeting him as her loving husband, she was dismayed and she scolded him: "If this kind of intensity of love and effort had been applied to your spiritual upliftment, you would be liberated by now."

At this comment Tulsidas felt as though he had been struck, for his ego was hit hard – and yet he realized that she was right in her wisdom. He vowed that he would not return until he had reached liberation. No longer a smitten lover, he focused totally on his sadhana and finally did return to His wife, who became His first disciple. She had realized the futility of her passionate husband's action and that human passion is a very unstable and unreliable companion.

When you get to know your body and your mind, you realize that the body cannot stand pain—pain which can also be infinite. The body cannot bear extreme pain, yet interestingly, it also cannot bear extreme pleasure. In both cases, the body will shatter. For example, the news of a sudden fortune or other highly pleasurable event can be so overwhelming that the heart simply cannot cope and manifests as a heart attack. Similarly, in the state of pain nothing is important; even the pain itself becomes unimportant. Nothing is important, no food, no clothing, no news, no friends or relations—nothing that may be going on in the world will matter. Whatever activity may have given you pleasure at one time, nothing is important any longer. Pain dominates your mind, but eventually you may become so fed up with the pain that you transcend the pain and achieve a more evolved state of mind.

Krishna explained to Arjuna: "I grant you the Divine Eye so you may see My Divine Nature – Who and What I am." In a similar manner, the *Satguru* will give you all the facilities, the new eye, the new body, for a complete renewal. Your perception can be changed and your mind altered positively.

Knowledge has existed since time immemorial. There have always been Teachers and there has always been Teaching throughout the world. No one can blame the fact that there was no opportunity for obtaining the sacred Knowledge, the manifestation of Truth. Throughout time, in various places, the Knowledge and the Teachers have always been available. Yet there have also always been betrayals of Truth. Well known in the ancient West, such as Greece, are Plato, Aristotle and Socrates, who all had very fine and sophisticated knowledge, highly influenced by the *Vedic* tradition. Later, others in Germany and France, including Hegel, Kant, Schopenhauer, Nietzsche and Voltaire, were similarly acknowledged. Yet, instead of utilizing and implementing this Knowledge, people betrayed the precious Higher Knowledge and the Universal Truth that had been offered. In the time of Jesus, people were given this sacred Knowledge, which was needed at that time, but when the opportunity came to prove that they were worthy of such Knowledge, manifesting strength and courage to face the evil, it was again betrayed. Often such Knowledge was passed from Teacher to Teacher underground, away from the general public, in order to preserve and safeguard it.

Ever since that time, there has been ongoing betrayal of Truth, in small ways and in big ways. Repeatedly, nations claim that other nations exploit and betray their culture. It seems that on one hand there is so much sacred Knowledge available, yet most of this falls prey to betrayal or misuse. Although there appears to be a universal longing for True Knowledge and Truth and many questions about life and the mystery of life, yet when the time comes, Truth is often discarded. It may be manipulated, controlled, misused and abused. What can never be blamed are the Teachings of Knowledge and Truth: these are always available for those who are ready. Those who are ready to seek will also find; and those who will knock will have the doors opened to them. The knocking is important—that you will have to do. Kabir says: "Your Beloved is waiting for you. Oh fool, open your curtain, the veil to see the Beloved sitting within you. Remove the veil, cast the clouding from your eye and clear your vision so you may behold the vision of the Beloved."

Kabir tells you that love is in your hand; you have been given the powerful and precious instrument of love which you can hold in your heart. This instrument is installed in you that you may become aware of Infinite Love. What you have been given you have been using very little: you need to utilize this gift to your utmost capacity. You have been given the mind to ponder the Knowledge and this pondering resembles digesting the Knowledge and making it part of yourself. Thus it becomes Living Knowledge. For instance, when you read books of Wisdom you cannot just read like you would a work of fiction. Each chapter contains so much Knowledge that you have to take it very slowly – maybe just a few lines at a time – then allow time for contemplation on the message given. Only when you have fully understood and digested what you have read should you continue.

You have been given a wonderful heart and an excellent mind and you can create your own wonderful world. Do not let anyone influence or dissuade you – especially someone not on the Path who may wish to give you advice about something he or she has no understanding of. There is a tendency for people like that to pull you into their level of understanding so that they can feel satisfaction. They may act from their emotional level, and this may stem from a kind of jealousy or, at other times, they may just wish to destroy what they cannot understand. That kind of confrontation is your test, indicating how far you have absorbed the Teachings and how strong you are to withstand this. It is part of this world's challenge to want to drag you down to a lower level. The Path you follow is the right Path: do not let anyone tell you that your Path is wrong. Right can never be wrong: wrong can never be right. Regard this Path as your precious treasure and let no one "steal" or demean it through their emotional imbalance.

6

Dialogues

Elements of nature, such as hot or cold, can certainly affect the working of your body as well as the workings of your mind. Maybe a cool or hot breeze on your face will touch you and, if you are sensitive, you will be able to notice the changes in the different elements within your body. The more intuitive you are, the more you will become aware of these changes. You will be aware of any change that may indicate a problem, such as an impending illness.

If you want to ask someone a question and you project an aggressive demeanor, it is not likely that you will get a good answer. If you really want to know some information, it is best to question the person in a more friendly attitude, without confrontation. Then, and more likely, you may get the desired information. Listening attentively is an important skill that is no longer very common.

Interestingly, when dealing with animals, while projecting a kind and caring vibration, animals will respond to you perfectly. Equally, they will perceive an aggressive and ill meaning attitude, like anger and dislike. An animal can actually notice this in the expression of your eyes; in fact the animal senses the energy from the look of your face. The communication between human beings, as well as communication between species, is very interesting. Messages can be conveyed without speech, without saying one word.

The emotional mechanisms of humans are very mysterious in a way. This can be seen in the example of Shiva and Uma. An ongoing dialogue is very important, whether between friends, couples, or within families. Of course, the traditional dialogue between Teacher and disciple is very special, unique and Divine. Such communication assists the disciple towards ongoing growth and bliss in the quest for liberation by removing the darkness of ignorance. Such dialogue is considered the Supreme Dialogue between the *Satguru* and the striving soul, as with Krishna and Arjuna and Ramakrishna Paramahansa and Vivekananda (previously Narendra) and Buddha and His *Rajguru* at the time of Buddha's marriage as Gautama.

The *Satguru* cannot easily find the evolving soul: He has to work with those souls who appear. Many seekers actually do not always need the Highest Knowledge; they may only require basic teaching. Nevertheless, a dialogue with the *Satguru* is always very special, and anyone availing themselves of the unique opportunity can experience a true spiritual dialogue.

In contrast to such spiritual dialogue, there are many countries and cultures where, in the evening after most of the day's work is over, people sit on their front steps and "watch the world go by." This is their way of relaxation after a hard day's work. It is also the perfect time to discuss the events of the day and, naturally, this also invites all the local gossip and chat. Not much may be going on, but anything unusual will be discussed at great length. In the big cities, people may be sitting in outdoor cafes or teashops, sipping their beverages, and, equally, they "watch the world go by" while discussing the latest interests or events.

If you are a more aware person on the spiritual Path, you will look at this type of interaction with Knowledge: you know the world and its habits and you do not get caught or engaged. On the lower level this is just passing the time – some entertainment. But that has no real benefit; at the most it is merely unproductive entertainment. Contemplative observation however – watching situations – can actually lead to inner insight. You may observe the bees and the butterflies and any other animals around and you start thinking about the many complexities of life. Bird watching in many countries has become a great tradition – apparently this is a residual quest for Knowledge. The idea is to observe and to analyze, to become a neutral observer. When you attach yourself to circumstances with any kind of emotion you will be caught in the process. Only when you can observe and detach will you not feel involved. There is a definite difference between merely observing and getting involved in the process.

Ongoing dialogue is a good habit. That is why the practice of *satsang* should be encouraged as a beautiful way of connecting with the Divine. It literally means "association with Truth." When people get together to listen or discuss and contemplate Divine Teachings, that is *satsang*. However, when you get together to just gossip, it is anything but *satsang*.

Rather than go through the endless discussion of someone wanting to do or not to do something, I will ask that person to tell me exactly what it is they want and I will adjust within that framework. I will genuinely try to help you and support you within the parameters of spiritual laws. But you must be truthful. That is very important: you have to be very honest and clear. Any pretense must be abandoned because you will continue to make a series of mistakes. It is like mathematics: if your original premise is wrong, if you make one original mistake, whatever you build thereafter can never stand and the final result will always be wrong.

There is nothing wrong with telling the truth about what you want. Let us say that someone wants to have all the worldly pleasures, as well as spiritual energy. There is nothing wrong with that. You would have to work out what percentage of spiritual energy you want – as long as you are clear in your perception. The problem arises when you are not truthful with yourself. If you can present your plan truthfully, that is fine and you can build a solid life upon that. The common mistake is that people may have all kinds of desires but do not admit to those. Instead there will be guilt, anger, defensiveness and justification – all kinds of negative emotions will start playing havoc with you. This is very important to remember; since you are living your life, do you not want to make it smooth, pleasant and fulfilling?

In life you need to assess what resources you have and ask yourself: "What are my capabilities, my aspirations and my goals?" You need to be clear about what you actually want. In the management of life, it does not matter at what stage you find yourself, whether as a young student, a middle-aged householder or older retired person. In the case of a retired person who is coming to the end of his or her natural lifespan, it is important to nurture contentment, happiness and having a feeling of fulfillment at all times.

It is so sad to witness that in some older people there remains bitterness relating to unresolved conflicts with family and friends – still blaming and complaining. What does it matter at this stage? Do you think about that? Is it not better to close all the disturbing chapters of years gone by, if possible by means of a long overdue dialogue with the person concerned? After thus clearing the air, you can focus on what makes you happy and how to enjoy life, while preparing for the next transition. With such positivity and amiability, you will be preparing the ground for your next life. Your evolution and progress continues. Who knows, it can even be possible that Enlightenment can be reached before you leave your body – when you are in that kind of spirit of happiness at the point of transition. There is a promise by the Divine Principle that at whatever stage you find yourself at the end of your life, that will be the deciding factor for your next life. It is a fundamental Divine Guarantee. In those circumstances, and if you are attuned with the *Satguru* and Highest Consciousness, liberation is guaranteed. If you are attuned with happiness and fulfillment, then you will definitely be happy in your next life. You will be born into circumstances where you have every opportunity to evolve and grow easily.

One possibility to prepare for end of life consciousness is to set up and present something like a "Golden Retreat," with the focus on offering some ideas and discussions for people to think in a way that will further their effort to evolve, rather than living daily in bitterness and unhappiness – and in the past – with thoughts of blame and guilt. This could be a truly helpful dialogue to prepare for transition. You have to understand also that you really do not have to wait for death – in any case, it will come. Yet there is also the question of whether you are ready to face death, whether you are ready to move on, while being prepared on all levels as a matter of normal transition.

In the meantime, at every stage of your life, you can plan your life as you actually wish it to manifest – even taken in short time increments – such as: over the next five years I will focus on my spiritual growth by following these practices and maintaining these thoughts, etc. The important aspect is not to fall into an abyss of negativity, which can disconnect you from spiritual understanding and your spiritual source. Spiritual disconnection is very serious.

The point is, you have complete freedom to grow as fast and far as you wish. You can dedicate your entire life to doing daily *sadhana* or you can do as much as you can through *seva*, meditation and spiritual reading. The important point is to make some kind of progress, even if it is just very small, rather than getting stuck or even sliding back into negative life patterns. You can set up a flexible spiritual plan for your life. As long as you are moving and growing and are not caught in darkness, frustration and depression, you are on the right Path. It is not difficult to discover what is right or wrong, what is helpful or a hindrance. The meter for assessment – your internal dialogue – is always there within you, as long as you pay attention to its prompts.

When dealing with day to day problems, especially when dealing with any kind of officialdom, you have to understand that many times you are also dealing with the kind of minds that have no imagination and frequently no problem solving skills – or even a desire to solve a problem. No dialogue will help in these circumstances – when the mind of one party is totally closed. There is no point at all in becoming disturbed: you are not going to change those minds. You have to accept who and what they are and try to work around the problems to find some solution. If you allow yourself to get drawn into that kind of argument or discussion that has no chance of resolving itself, people can often get so angry that they can become physical, resulting in having to deal with the repercussions of that behavior.

Instead, it is very helpful to have an ongoing dialogue with your inner self to keep you on track. You could compare it

7

Wild Mind and Gentle *Viveka*

Opening Meditation: *Make yourself comfortable and sit quietly. Gently close your eyes and just focus on your breathing for a moment. Breathe slowly and gently, not thinking about anything, just watching your breath going in and out. Let your mind be empty and quiet. Any thoughts that come, let them just pass by, pay no attention to thoughts. Watch the movement in the body, breathing slowly, there is nothing to worry about, nothing to do, no reason to hurry, just enjoy the sensation.*

When your mind is relaxed, you are relaxed; when your mind is at peace you are at peace; when your mind is calm, you are calm. Your mind interacts with your body, your senses and your emotions.

There is a traditional meditation where the soul is speaking to the mind, or *Viveka*, the wise intellect, is speaking to your mind (Mind). Consider Mind as a wild man and *Viveka* as his gentle and wise female companion. The Wild Man Mind is always engaged in doing wild and often crazy things and Gentle Female Companion *Viveka* is always telling him to calm down. She tells him: "*Ramji karenge beda par − udas man kahe ko dare −* Oh, distressed mind, why do you worry? The Supreme Beloved will take you across the ocean of suffering and pain. Why do you fear?"

Thus the wise *Viveka* tells the mind not to be concerned:

"Your boat will be taken across the ocean. That ocean is the visible and invisible world infested with all kinds of dangers: anger, greed, obsession, possession, desires, selfishness, self-centeredness, envy, jealousy, guilt, regret, depression, frustration, conditioning of mind, action and reaction, the list is endless. These are only the inner enemies; additionally there are the many outer negative forces creating waves within this ocean. You can see how difficult it can be to swim across.

Only when you are brave, self-assured and have taken refuge at the lotus feet of the Divine Beloved, then: "*Ramji karenge bede par – udas man kahe ko dare* – the Supreme Beloved will take you across the ocean, the *samsara*."

You can use this kind of meditation at any time, especially when you may be feeling depressed or low. When low energy manifests it will continue to pull you down, especially, when your Sun energy is low. There are several kinds of Sun energy: the spiritual, the physical, the emotional and the medical Sun energy. The medical Sun energy you may get in capsule form in many different unit levels. This is known as Vitamin D. Essentially all vitamins available are originally from nature: Earth energy, Sun energy, tree energy, and plant and flower energy. Be careful though: know what you are doing and get your physician's advice on the dosage. More of anything is not always better, such as in the case of obsessive or possessive emotion. Only true, spontaneous care can never be too much – it does not expect anything.

The body, being a most wonderful "machine," is also able to produce all that is required: nourishment for the physical, emotional and spiritual needs. The body is a marvelous piece of work – a masterpiece of creation, perfect in every sense. Nevertheless, despite all its wonderful capabilities, the body can also manifest as ugly and demonic. It is stated that some demons incarnate in human form to create chaos and confusion and to inflict pain and suffering. Those are very real demonic forces living in human bodies. That is why the world is in so much trouble through war, destruction, terrorism, killings, and murder – all created by the human being.

Whenever nature creates an incident, it becomes a big lesson for humans to learn and to set things right. There are two aspects of disaster: individual and collective. An individual disaster is a sign that there is something not quite right with you, around you or within you. It is a warning and it is a lesson to learn. This should be heeded rather than blaming or complaining that you have not done anything wrong. How do you know that you have done nothing wrong? It seems everyone is convinced that they are doing right and have never done wrong. Hardly anyone will admit that they have done wrong.

Remember that any time there is a misfortune, whether physical, emotional, psychological or psychical – or any other trouble or disaster – it is a message or warning. The warning means that there is something in your life you have to set right. Similarly, when there is a disaster in the world, like the recent torrential downpour in the Himalayas or a tsunami, it is a warning for humanity as a whole that whatever they are doing, something is not right. It is a warning from nature, from the cosmic forces to the collective humanity.

During the time of the *Ramraj*, the Golden Age, the Supreme Age, no one suffered. No one owned anything, yet everyone had what they needed. When Krishna built the kingdom of *Dvaraka*, He provided everything and everything belonged to everyone. Everything was available in abundance: there was no need for money, no buying or selling – all your needs were met and there was no need to store anything.

There are two major traditional concepts of a society: one is *Ramraj*, the Kingdom of *Rama*, the Golden Age, and the other is *Dvaraka*, the Divine Kingdom of *Krishna*. The many thousand devotees and companions were given equal status: there was no hierarchy. Everything was perfect: no disease, no pain, and no need of anything. Every day was a celebration; people awakened in happiness and went to sleep feeling happy in a semi-meditative state with wonderful dreams. Dreams can be like that; some are so beautiful that you do not even want to wake up and do not care for wakeful consciousness. The dream can be so pleasant that you want to dream forever and you may feel upset when you awaken. That, however, is also a lesson: you can create your life so that such a dream can happen again and again and you can return to a dreamlike state naturally.

On the other hand, there are also dreams that can be called "nightmares." Sometimes you may dream that you have signed some important agreement and later you discover that this was a big mistake, but when you wake up you are relieved – the danger has been averted, it is no longer valid! In dreams you may be in deep trouble but when you awaken in daytime reality, the relief that you are "out of danger" is a wonderful feeling. Actually, you never were in danger, except that the state of danger had been created for you by the mind. When you dismiss a dream as "just a dream," you forget that this is another state of consciousness, a state of sub-consciousness, which is equally real. Yet when you awaken you dismiss it. The point is that there is an element of learning in all of this. In a way, you cannot separate dreams from nightmares; both dreams and nightmares are real, just on a different level of consciousness. You can create a nightmare while in wakeful consciousness and you can also create a dreamlike state in the wakeful consciousness. Many things are at your command if you follow the right balanced Path. You can listen to this wild and mad mind and you can waste twenty precious years of time – lost years. You can also listen to *Viveka* – Wisdom – and you can be happy, integrating all your happiness into your life. The choice is yours.

Some people consider a so-called "good life" as "living the dream." Amassing goods and some wealth and maybe some power is often regarded as "living the dream." Unfortunately, this type of material dream often includes the tendency to overstate your personal material success and to regard others of lesser means as inferior. This is merely another sign of a distorted mind.

When Mind plays with you and tells you that you are better because you have more outer resources or achievements than others, it is nothing but mind playing tricks on you. Mind is tricking you all the time, telling you that you are superior to others or, conversely, that you are inferior to others. We talked about the Wild Man Mind and his Gentle, Wise Female Companion Viveka. That Wild Man Mind will play with you and trick you time and again. Instead, try to listen to the gentle and wise Viveka. She will tell you that you are neither superior nor inferior: you are what you are, the Supreme Self, part of the Whole.

When you forget that reality and real Truth, you become lost in the ocean of distorted emotion. There is nothing wrong in enjoying what presents itself, but you should remember that you are not your enjoyment: it is only a passing phase. Nothing will last forever: everything has a temporary application.

There is also no point in a High Being teaching you the whole day. There is only so much that you are able to digest. Consider what you learn here as when you were taught in a class: you also have to do homework. After that, you will have to produce the results for assessment. The point is you need to have time to reflect, contemplate and absorb the Teachings. If I were to teach you the whole day, it does not mean you will become more evolved. Reflection and "digestion" of the Teachings are very important.

Previously, I gave the example of the cow where the digestive process goes through four different stomachs. Indian tradition has always revered the cow for its many outstanding qualities. It is easily domesticated, needing relatively little maintenance except a good place to graze, shelter from the elements, perhaps some cleansing and regular milking. After grazing, the half-chewed grass is stored in the rumen of the cow and that is the most important part of the digestion. The cow sits comfortably and just munches away. She looks relaxed as though in meditation. Mentally this is what you need to do with the given Knowledge: you need to "ruminate" on the Wisdom. Further along, separation of nutrients and waste products takes place in the reticulum and omasum of the cow, until finally the nutrients for nourishment and energy are absorbed into the bloodstream from the final stomach, the abomasum. This energy is also transmuted into milk – and milk in abundance – as a gift to humanity since the cow produces far more than the little calf can drink. We take much of these wonderful designs of nature for granted, rarely considering the true miracle of nature's working. We are surrounded by miracles but generally pay little or no attention to them – until something goes wrong.

The point is that when Knowledge is asked for and given,

how much can you actually receive, digest and implement? This question is like being asked to carry fifty kilos when you have difficulty carrying five kilos. Of course, you want to try everything, learn everything, practice everything, and follow everything. By way of example, this is similar to being in a train station where many trains are ready to leave. Only one of them is the superfast, high-speed and luxurious train. Yet often people like to take the slower passenger trains that stop at every little village and go on little detours through the countryside. Unfortunately, when they have had enough of "looking around," they find that the fast train has gone. When you have a majestic river like the Indian Ganga near you, why would you want to bathe in a miserable ditch? When you live near the ocean, why swim in a swimming pool? The same principle applies to food shopping. You may have a clean, well-run shop that specializes in healthy and organic foods, and then there are twenty others, maybe not so clean, with cheap food full of preservatives that cause you sickness.

These are just simple examples in life; the point is you have to give your choices some thought. Many times one does not recognize what one gets, continuing to look for this and that, going here and there. The mystic poet saint Kabir says: "I am with you here and yet you are searching all over." Remember this and allow the Grace of *Viveka* to be present as a priority.

8

Bacteria and Viruses

Humans have a tendency to think that they are the most powerful species in life and superior to all other living organisms on earth. This is not so. Do not underestimate the power of bacteria and viruses: they may be so small that a human eye cannot see them, but their powerful effect cannot be ignored. The so-called "superior" human being can easily become the victim of the tiniest little organism. Superiority implies that you are so strong and resistant that nothing unwanted can happen to you. Yet when you are subject to injuries and illness, one bite of a tiny mosquito can infect you and you can be faced with years of suffering or even death. Human beings are so vulnerable that any sense of arrogance is inappropriate. Just put a person inflated with ego into a closed room and throw in a few mosquitoes – then watch what happens. It is important to remember that no creature is inferior.

The human ego is like a balloon; one little prick with a needle and it deflates completely. Then what happens to all the labels you have attached to yourself: I am rich, I am powerful, I am clever, I am beautiful, I am so talented and I am famous? It is all meaningless. All of those labels can vanish like the air in the balloon.

Even plant pollen can disturb and even cause havoc in the human system: those minute yellow particles of powder can make people feel so ill and weak that they feel incapable of going about their daily activities. In extreme cases where people have a compromised respiratory system or other sensitivities, pollen sensitivity can lead to a health crisis and even death, regardless of how strong they think they are. On the other hand, if you are spiritually evolved and resistant to many externals, your body, mind and heart will be different.

Ego is generally nothing but an illusion based on identification with social standing, occupation, religious denomination or political power. Even personal appearance seems to be one of the biggest preoccupations of the human ego. People are not what they think they are and in the name of ego people often do terrible things to each other: history is full of such examples. Actually we do not need to look at history since the daily media provides countless daily examples of the atrocities humans commit on one another – and all because of the vanity and illusion of the false ego. People build up a life of make-believe; they start believing what is not true and act on that basis.

On the one hand there is illusion and on the other hand there is Knowledge. In the morning, when the sun rises, your understanding may also be clear. Yet during the day you become caught in the web of *Maya*, in the illusion of this world. I see the *lila* every day when people sacrifice the Highest Knowledge for the lowest desires. The majority of humanity is subject to this delusion. When you are deluded you feel that do not have to deal with this life. Many people's minds have been influenced and affected with countless drugs – both prescription and otherwise. People go into the hospital and are often given more drugs. When they come out, they may not know where they are or what they are doing and they are certainly not themselves. Drugs can create a chemical reaction in the body and further pollute mind and soul.

In contrast, powerful True Knowledge will also create a chemical reaction in your system which is conducive to your happiness, growth, bliss and balance. Interestingly, both methods create a powerful yet very different chemical reaction in your system. The brain gives instructions to the senses, to be happy or to be unhappy; it is telling your senses how to behave. For instance it is the brain that sends the message that there is pain. Essentially pain is just a message from the brain, but an evolved brain can mitigate all pain, whether physical, mental or emotional. The brain can direct the organs and the senses: feel pain or feel pleasure. Organs and senses are actually the "slaves" of the brain. When you receive some impression, that impression will transmit the impulses to the brain and the brain then decides how to react. It may say: "laugh now" and so you laugh; or "cry now" and you will cry. Only spiritual evolution can make you the master of your brain and its sensitive functioning, when your mind becomes more highly tuned and passes the order or instruction to the brain with a much greater level of understanding.

Most thoughts in the modern world are focused on material advantages as well as on sensual pleasures and how to get the most out of those pleasures – sense perception. The spiritual – *Adhyatmik* – Path however provides much more than ordinary joy – bliss. Bliss is generally connected with the soul, whereas pleasure is connected with the senses. The modern way of living is primarily a pleasure-seeking path. Many religious doctrines are focused on desire-seeking prayers – often incorporating requests into prayers – on the basis of some flattery to the relevant deities or gods. The world culture seems to embrace a desire-seeking formula.

Vedic philosophy teaches overcoming the desire for pleasures to reach Enlightenment. This Knowledge cannot be compared to any other knowledge. Pleasure-seeking consciousness reveals a much lower level of consciousness. Striving for spiritual fulfillment and Enlightenment is very different and when you are Enlightened, everything is transformed.

According to *Vedic* philosophy, *Maya* – the world of illusion – is so strong that time and again people get caught. They create a trap for themselves and get caught in that trap. They believe they know what is good for them and become caught. Only an objective mind can discern what is truly good or right. As long as you have a subjective mind you can never be sure what is good for you. But that instinct is so powerful and negative that it will influence the positive.

The play of *Maya* with all her tricks and temptations is so very interesting: remember the story of the two boys, Krishna and Sudama who, during a rainstorm, were caught in the forest with very little to eat. Sudama, the older boy, had been given some chickpeas by their *Guru* mother to share between them. Although now in charge of the handful of chickpeas, Sudama became very aware of his hunger and covertly ate the chickpeas without giving any to the young Krishna under the pretext that he, Sudama, could not afford to feel "weak" while guiding the younger boy out of the forest. While secretly eating, the chickpeas made a cracking noise and Krishna, the Divine Mind, although knowing exactly what was happening, asked what the noise was. Sudama lied, stating that it was his teeth chattering in the cold. This lie and the "sin" of leaving the younger boy hungry and cold while filling his own stomach, had devastating *karmic* results for Sudama. He became a pauper and most of his life suffered for that stupid, reckless mistake. Eventually Sudama had to petition Krishna for help many years later in adulthood.

This is just one example which illustrates how negative impulses can literally overtake your mind and your life. Unfortunately, people do not see that necessarily. That is why they need a Teacher to tell them and explain the Truth. But then again, they may not like to hear the Truth they are being told.

9

Dharma and *Adharma*

There is a *Sanskrit* word called *"chaitanya"* – you could call it "awareness." One who understands or knows the reality and is spiritually aware is called *chaitanya*. The *Upanishads* recommend that each individual should be so aware that they become *chaitanya*.

According to the spiritual tradition, the term *"chaitanya"* refers to someone with all-around awareness. Interestingly, all animals and small creatures are in the category of being *chaitanya*: it is an inbuilt quality. When observing an animal, a dog for instance, you can see that it is totally aware within its own world. It may not be able to read or write, but it is still *chaitanya*. This kind of awareness manifests automatically, like doing things automatically: you could liken it to the programming of a robot. Essentially, the vast majority of people live their lives according to their conditioning, starting in childhood. In some way there is a resemblance to the functioning of the robot, except that humans do have a choice to think and to re-program themselves by using their discretion.

Nowadays, there is a strong debate about creating robotic "helpers" and in a way it could be quite useful. The robot is programmed and will do as instructed – unquestioning and without arguing, complaining or asking for explanations. It simply has its job description and will execute the required tasks:

cleaning, mopping, cooking, making tea, presenting refreshment on a tray and much more. It may not be human, but it has some human touch!

Dealing with the human is fine, but it can also be very complicated and protracted since humans have a very complex mind mechanism. A robot does not feel insulted; it does not sulk, does not "go on strike," does not have emotional outbursts, and does not burn your toast in revenge! In contrast, human beings can get upset about the simplest things. Meanwhile, a pet dog for instance, knows its duty and does it perfectly – as does a cat by discouraging insects and small creatures.

It is interesting to observe that in nature, every animal, plant and all others are doing their jobs very effectively. They have been given their particular task and are carrying it out efficiently and without deviation – that is their *dharma*.

The human life, however, is different. It is the only life that provides an exit from the wheel of *samsara*, from the bondage of the perpetual cycle of life, death and rebirth: from the bondage of ignorance, darkness and negativity. Although considered to be the only state of attaining that freedom from the cycle of rebirth, it can also become an imprisonment, depending on whether one is following one's own *dharma*. *Dharma* will ensure that you walk on the right Path of duty and responsibility, of right effort, right speech and right deed. Unfortunately, some are following the path of *adharma*, which is the opposite of *dharma*. When following the Path of *dharma*, this will eventually lead to your final liberation. However, when following the opposite path of *adharma*, this does not lead towards freedom of the soul, but rather the imprisonment of soul. Interestingly, the human life presents both, extreme development and evolution, as well as the confinement of oneself to ignorance and darkness.

Considering the many creatures in the world with their set job description or established role, the human being differs in the sense that they have choices. They can endeavor to do and be what they choose. The saying that "you can be what you want to be" is perfectly true in that sense. At the same time, human beings are also controlled by so many forces, which are partly created by themselves and partly by others.

Divine effort resembles a plane as it takes off using great force, lifting up, breaking free of the clouds and moving smoothly into the clear sky. Life is generally full of turbulence and turmoil. At every corner or stage, something or someone may be "lurking" to create an uninvited and unexpected challenge.

People ask many questions, one of which arises frequently: How can one avoid crisis and conflict? Is it even possible to avoid crisis and conflict? In principle, the answer is yes, one can live life without crisis and conflict. In practice, however, it appears almost impossible, partly because of one's own understanding, as well as the understanding of others. The understanding and concept of life, the many cultural mores reflected in day to day living, vary enormously, as do people's perceptions of each other. Such factors make it very difficult to avoid crises and conflicts.

Evolved beings have no conflicts, turmoil and crises, for they do not identify with the issues of any crisis, whereas the normal human being keeps identifying with almost all crises. That is why if one had a robot and one told the robot that this time the tea is not good enough, the robot will be reassuring: "Very well Master, I will improve," without having its ego hurt. But if one confronts a human being with this criticism, the reaction would be very different: they might respond by suggesting that someone else should take over to make the tea. Thus a simple issue can turn into a conflict.

Emotional issues regularly surface. Human beings often conduct themselves emotionally. For example, improving a tried and tested recipe further by adding more of a special ingredient does not always turn out to be an improvement. Generosity in giving more is not always an improvement. In the same vein, ongoing concern toward another person can sometimes manifest or be perceived to be nagging. Many times, what one thinks is right is not always right. The point is not to rely on the perception of what is right, rather ensure that it is right in a detached manner.

Humans are complex beings – like machines with countless inbuilt emotions that act, react and interact constantly. Maybe that is why the policy of "stick and carrot" evolved in many places and in different ways. Sometimes the carrot of positive enforcement will work and at other times there may be the need of a stick-reprimand. Occasionally however, too little carrot and too much stick can also backfire, or become ineffective.

When talking about crises and turmoil in life, it is helpful to remember the quotation by the poet saint Kabir: "Everyone will invoke Divine Energy when in trouble." People pray when unexpected trouble comes, when in conflict, when suffering or in pain. Imagine being on an airplane and the plane is in difficulty; praying or repeating a *mantra* with the hope of averting a problem in such a desperate situation is a natural response. The same applies to everyday life problems when unexpected trouble comes that seems overwhelming, such as being faced with a huge income tax bill, having failed an important exam or having an accident. The point is that when sudden problems arise, that is when people tend to remember the Divine.

Kabir says that when life itself resembles a prayer — a decent, good and helpful life — and when people follow the *dharma*, there will be no need for an emergency call asking for Divine Intervention. First of all, in that case trouble is not likely to appear. Secondly, if by chance it does come, by the time it may be effective it will just disperse. Compare this to being like a sun: when an icy meteorite approaches, it will melt. Therefore, if one's deeds are good deeds, if one is following the *dharma*, if one's life is filled with prayer and meditation, and one has the *Satguru's* Grace and protection, it is unlikely that one will have any real trouble. Any dark cloud that tries to darken your horizon will disappear before it can actually be effective. Just as a tornado from afar appears to be extremely dangerous at maximum speed and capacity, when under Divine protection, as it comes closer, the power dissipates. It all depends on one's lifestyle and *karmic* engagement. If one follows the path of *adharma*, when trouble strikes, and one wants to take refuge in prayer, this may not be possible.

When people become ill or meet with an unfortunate incident — for instance, they get a diagnosis of a serious and potentially life-threatening disease — that is the time many want to change their lifestyle with healthy food, exercise and positive thinking. Only at the point of potential disaster will a change of their previous negative habits become important. Well, sometimes this works but other times it may be just too late. Life does not work like that. One cannot undo the damage caused by a lifetime of wrong living, having poisoned and polluted body and mind, in a few months.

Many times the issue of pollution is directly related to human greed, such as spreading pesticides to get a larger crop of produce, thereby poisoning the people who consume such foods.

In a country with very large hungry populations where getting enough food is a priority, the focus is often not the health of the people, but rather on the goal of big companies to make money. Health becomes an afterthought – if at all. Maybe this could be described as collective *adharma*.

The contamination or poisoning of food for profit throughout the world is shocking. Pesticides are one of the major global problems. More and more people exhibit strong allergic or ill reactions as a result. Ideally, everyone should have a patch of land to grow their own organic vegetables and food to balance the collective *tamasic* influence.

We talk of crisis, trouble and turmoil, and with the normal human being there always seems to be some trouble for the human being. But it is exactly the human who has the capability and the choice to either increase or to reduce it. It is said that "Knowledge makes you free," and those fortunate enough to have received spiritual Knowledge also have the Knowledge and capability to steer their lives through any kind of crisis. The vast proportion of suffering, individual or collective, is based on nothing more than ignorance and absence of mindfulness. There are countless situations where the mind alone creates endless pain, suffering and conflict.

All this can be avoided and eliminated. In India, people have devised a way of catching monkeys. Knowing that monkeys love peanuts, people fill a narrow-necked container with peanuts and place it where monkeys often come. As one monkey approaches, it pushes its hand through the narrow neck into the container, greedily grabs a fistful and finds its hand trapped. It cannot withdraw the hand while holding the nuts. Now, if the monkey were to let go of the peanuts, it could easily remove its hand and free itself, but the monkey's greed overcomes its safety. It remains hopelessly caught in its ignorance of not letting go to regain its freedom. There are many examples of people putting their hands in places where they can get really hurt.

There is nothing either bad or good in this world: it depends on how one deals with it − in one's mind. It is not so simple to classify right and wrong. Everything depends on the working of the mind and related factors. Look at the example of filth or dirt: it could be used as fertilizer to make things grow yet it can also harbor deadly bacteria that can create horrible diseases and suffering. It is society that creates the labels of "bad" and "good." It is the usage, how something is used, that makes it bad or good. Of all the negative forces, even ego and anger can be productive at times if they prevent some disaster or create positive change. This is certainly a constructive application of emotion. All emotions are forces for appropriate use.

Unfortunately people have been taught to believe in the concept of bad and good. The application of energy however, is the only thing that matters, the only thing that makes it good or bad. Consider the use of the element uranium − it is a tremendous source that can be used to provide energy for the world and it can also destroy the entire world. Sugary sweets may be very delicious but can also cause major health problems. Substances called "poison" can have healing properties. Drugs may give temporary pleasure, but long-term use can be destructive. All depends on use or abuse. Technology has advanced to a degree that almost everyone can learn to handle the internet with so much information, yet it can also be a cause for harm.

Once, all the land belonged to everyone. Many cultures, including Native Americans for instance, had no concept of "owning" land. Being much more attuned to the laws of nature, the land was there for everyone to use as the bounty of Mother Earth. When the greedy "land grabbers" came, they put up the signs "No Trespassing – trespassers will be shot." That was the end of living within the laws of nature and *adharma* was evident. Greed has not diminished since then – rather it has increased in all forms. There are a few countries that still try to follow the law of nature whenever possible, but these examples are reducing each year.

The law of nature is different from the law of man and when the law of man contradicts the law of nature, the law of nature will always prevail and the law of man will always be defeated. That is the Supreme Law – none is stronger. Unfortunately humans do not understand. One has to understand and align with nature. When one aligns one's life, work, and deeds, living life within the concepts of *dharma*, then nature will actually be protective like a Mother.

10

Living in *Purnatirth* and *Dvaraka*

Generally known as the seat of the Kingdom of Krishna, the concept of *Dvaraka* is meaningful on many levels. The *Sanskrit* term *dvar* refers to "the door" – it is the door to bliss or true Krishna Consciousness or Krishna *Loka*. That is the meaning of *Dvaraka*. Opening that door, the only experience is bliss: it is the door to Higher Knowledge and joy, a place where there is no misery, no suffering, no pain. Everything is beautiful and full of love, peace and prosperity.

That same *Dvaraka* is also present in everybody's heart. Although it does not exist physically any more, there used to be a real "Kingdom of Krishna" which dissolved into the sea when Krishna left. As times changed and people's consciousness declined to a lower level, *Dvaraka* decided to sink and to dissolve back into the sea whence it had come. There was no purpose in its continued existence without Krishna Awareness.

A place where a High Being and Divine manifestation has played the *lila* becomes a *tirth*. There is now a place we named "*Purnatirth*." However, in order to maintain the spiritual *Purnatirth* vibration, you have to be in the appropriate frame of mind. When you go to *Purnatirth*, you have to leave all your negativity behind. Leave all these negative attributes behind before you enter. You enter the place with love, with reverence, and respect, remembering the *Satguru* and His Energy. Only then can you maintain the real *Purnatirth* vibration. But, if you go to *Purnatirth* with all the emotional and mental baggage that you have accumulated, you will not feel the spiritual energy and vibration. It is very easy to forget where you are and whom you are with, taking the *Satguru* for a normal human being and forgetting His Divine attributes. While it is helpful to be relaxed, one should not forget with Whom one is and maintain humility and devotion.

If the *Satguru* comes down to your level, that does not mean that you can treat Him like anybody else. It is through the *Satguru's* generosity and kindness that He comes down to the lowest level to deal with, to interact and to play with people for the sole purpose of communicating the spiritual message of upliftment and the dissemination of Divine Knowledge. Do not treat the *Satguru* like any other human being. He may be the best and truest friend you will ever have, but He is not one of your casual contacts or family members. It is fine to be relaxed and easy, but not so relaxed that your feet are on the chair – so that your very posture becomes a sign of disrespect. One example of positive behavior can be seen with babies. A baby likes to hold your finger very tightly – that is his or her security. It is very interesting that the baby feels secure and safe by simply holding your finger. Now consider holding the finger of the Divine; you feel safe and secure by holding that Divine finger tightly. Do not let it slip. Remember also that this hold does not work unless you are attuned. When you take an instrument and you want to create a sound, you have to be in harmony, in tune, with the sound of the instrument.

Therefore, whenever you go to *Purnatirth*, go with devotion, dedication and humility. Remember the Teaching, remember the Divine *Lila*, and remember all the nice things that have happened to you. This will help to uplift you to that level of consciousness, and that is the way to attune to Higher Energy. On that basis you will benefit whenever you go to *Purnatirth*. You will recreate the *lila*, the *satsang* vibration and energy, provided that you go with a pure mind, free from all negativity.

Wherever a High Being disseminates the Teaching, that place becomes a *tirth*. *Tirth* is where the Divine *Lila* is played. Why do people go to Rishikesh, Benares, or Vrindavan? These are the places where High Beings, *Satgurus*, emitted Divine Energy. Without Buddha, Bodhgaya is nothing. Without Ganga, Rishikesh is nothing. With High Beings, Ganga is sacred. Ganga was asked: "Oh Ganga, how do you relieve your suffering, your pain, which you have taken from the millions when they dip down and leave their sins behind?" Ganga replied: "When a High Being walks by, and I kiss His Feet – that is how I relieve my pain and suffering." You can therefore imagine how important the Feet of a High Being, the Feet of the *Satguru*, are.

You have to understand that you must open your heart to connect. If your heart is filled with weeds, how can you expect flowers to grow? When filled with weeds and thorns, the thorns' duty is to pierce. Unfortunately, when some people open their mouth to speak, it can actually feel like a bite. Every word can "bite" you to the point that you want to run away. In contrast, someone who is evolving and positive – every word of his or hers can be like nectar. You manifest what you have in your heart: if you grow thorns, how can you bring out flowers? Purity of heart is very important, and only possible when you connect to the Divine Play, to the Divine *Lila*, and to Divine Knowledge.

Recently someone asked how to prevent infection from injuries. Of course, you can apply some soothing lotion. But if you want a total cure, there is no panacea for everything. Only one thing – Divine Love, Divine Energy – will bring about a total cure. When your mind is filled with Divine Energy and Love, then all organs, all senses, all parts of your body and mind will be filled with the healing energy and function in harmony. That is called "body healing." When you are healthy and happy, you will make others happy too.

I have spoken about the mind or Mind. I gave an example that you can live for many years not realizing that you are in misery. Yet the most fascinating thing about the mind is that it can justify the misery. That is actually the most shocking thing. For twenty years you may suffer and you say: "Oh no, no – I did not suffer!" Is that not amazing? You may have gone through physical pain and mental pain and deny that you alone have caused the suffering by your mind, and you could have chosen a positive alternative, but your ego says: "No, it was nothing." That kind of assessment is truly amazing. After all, what could be more shocking than the mind justifying all your suffering? It is also an attribute of strength, emphasizing your power of endurance. If this power were for the special purpose of your *sadhana*, you would be on the Path to Enlightenment. However, harnessing power to endure the darkness is actually frightening. It is not correct to consider having the power of endurance for pain and suffering a strength or virtue.

This is actually a classic example of how you imprison your soul. Endurance should be for the sake of the Higher Purpose. Parvati decided that Shiva was all She wanted, and She went through tremendous hardships to reach Shiva. But when your *sankalpa*, power, your determination, is to enable your negative mind to prevail, you are not persisting for Divine Power. You are not saying "I am starving" for the sake of humanity;

you are not persisting for the sake of the *Satguru*. You want your limited desire to prevail.

Divine endurance bears fruit, plenty of fruit. You may be walking through deserts and mountains – for a humanitarian cause – experiencing all the pain and suffering and heat, until you nearly collapse, when finally, near death, you arrive at a cool oasis, with many fruits and a natural jacuzzi. You refresh yourself in the sparkling water, put on nice clean clothing, maybe even have a massage and have lots of people to attend to you. That kind of effort and endurance is worth it. Otherwise, why endure pain suffering and even torture – and for what? Ask yourself: ten, twenty years of suffering – for what? What did you achieve – nothing but an accumulation of negatives. If you had some cause, some purpose, then the greater fruit would be waiting for you: "I have done something – I have born torture, I have gone through penance, I have gone through all that for the sake of my spiritual growth." A *sadhu* may go through all the penance – extreme heat or extreme cold – and he has a purpose, an aim. He may be doing it for his *Satguru* or to overcome all attachments.

There has to be some aim, some purpose, for you to go through pain and suffering. For example, one day a disciple was cooking; it was very hot and, in addition, he had to cook on a very hot fire. The food he prepared was very much appreciated by everyone. However, he was so exhausted he could not enjoy the food himself. Now this is not a recommended practice, but since everybody else really enjoyed the food, he considered his effort well worth it – although it was not the intention to exhaust himself. Therefore, if you have no purpose to your suffering, beware of your negative mind. That mind can trick you into the most unproductive actions. When you go to *Purnatirth*, hold *Dvaraka* in your heart, or *Ramraj*, the Golden Kingdom of Rama, where everything was perfect. You can create these concepts within your heart, even during the dark times of *Kali Yuga*, and you can always carry the Knowledge with you.

During the time of the ideological divide between the East and the West in Europe, being caught as a spy and interrogated, maybe tortured, to provide certain information, was a big danger. It is said that the KGB tried to understand the *yogic* power for its own purposes. That is a good example: the *yogic* ability of thoughts stored in the mind is useful to prevent detection. Camera images or documents are far more easily detected and they can be taken as evidence with dire consequences. But how can anyone catch what is in your mind? How can anyone detect what is in your heart – your Knowledge and Wisdom? That is where the modern material world fails. In fact all systems fail, because what is in the heart can never be detected. Of course, torture can be used to make you confess anything. Torture has been used since the beginning of time, as well as currently. If spies received *yogic* training, they could train themselves to detach the mind from the body without ever feeling pain. The same applies to people who want to keep a secret and do not want anyone to discover their secret. The practice of *yogic* powers, to detach mind and emotion, would be of great benefit if used properly.

When you practice detachment from your negativity, like when you are asked to go to *Purnatirth* from time to time, it should not be difficult to just align yourself positively for a few hours or a few days – with a pure heart. Similarly, when a seeker travels to see their Teacher or *Satguru*, they are unaware of their surroundings as their focus is preparation for the *darshan*. It is possible, if your mind is attuned, to be in a different state of consciousness.

While in that altered state of consciousness, the mind

can replay an event or situation, especially when focused on the Divine *Lila*. During the time of Krishna, the *gopis*, cowgirls of Vrindavan, actually lived in that *lila*. Although ordinary girls, with their pure love, they could make the child Krishna dance for buttermilk. Yet, to a number of highly evolved souls who were longing to have just a glance of Krishna during their meditation, it was amazing that these simple girls could "bribe" Krishna to dance for them – for the sake of a little buttermilk. In fact, the purity of the *gopis'* love is so profound that this Being – powerful beyond human comprehension – this Supreme Being, Krishna, whom many advanced *yogis* are longing to comprehend for one minute, dances for these ordinary girls of Vrindavan.

Divine madness is different, because Divine madness leads to Enlightenment. You do not go around crazily and cause damage. That is not Divine madness. You do not do silly things. Divine madness creates beauty, song, dance, poetry, intoxication, and love affecting your heart and mind. Many mystical beings like Kabir or Mira have experienced Divine madness; they have created exquisitely beautiful philosophy in their so-called "madness." Mira, the Rajastani princess, was in love with Krishna, and she created such beautiful thoughts and songs that they still inspire millions today. Mira says: "My *Satguru* is my boat, the One who takes me across the ocean of suffering. He is the One who steers the boat. My boat is made of Truth and Love and the One who will take my boat across the ocean to the other side – that is my *Satguru*." Such Divine madness – Divine intoxication – creates Knowledge in your mind and love in your heart.

Beware of your mind. Create your own world. Create your own Divine Kingdom, with the help of the *Satguru*. You are so blessed and fortunate to have access to this Knowledge,

Grace and Divine Energy. Maybe you have done something in your last life to earn this privilege of awareness, and you are here to resume – in spite of any difficult environment. You are still trying, which is good; always carry on and keep trying. Never get caught in pessimism and hopelessness. It is very easy to get caught in all kinds of negativity. Someone may call you and tell you something really silly, and then you start doubting the whole spiritual quest. If that disturbs you, it means you still have a long way to go on your Path.

When you really practice spirituality, your determination becomes rock solid – not fickle and fleeting like little leaves that the slightest breeze can blow around. That is your strength; having received so much Knowledge and Wisdom, who should prevail in the world? You, who have done *satsang*, or some fickle negative mind caught in its own miserable life? Who should prevail? If you are not able to deal with simple and silly comments yourself, it is time to question your own ability and achievement. Having received considerable spiritual Knowledge and guidance, you should be able to deal with inappropriate comments. That is a very basic quality which you should have acquired. It is not fitting to bring simple and foolish gossip to the attention of the *Satguru*. Then what is the difference between those who are caught in this deep blue sea of *Maya*, and you who is supposed to have been inspired by Divine Knowledge? There should be some difference in your manifestation. Therefore, from time to time, do ask yourself, inquire and contemplate: "What have I achieved from listening to the Knowledge?" You have to be strong and steady to withstand the wayward winds that prevail in the world.

You can compare this to seasoned wood, wood which has been left exposed to the elements: heavy rain, snow, hot sun and any kind of weather and not just for one year, but for many years. Having been thus exposed, wood knows how to withstand torture and pain. Such wood is of the finest quality, beloved by artists, who can make beautiful carvings and statues from it. To learn to withstand the "weather of life," you have to go through the process of life so that you may become as solid as a rock or seasoned wood, yet with the flexibility of the wind, with the fragrance of a flower and the fluidity of water. When you develop these qualities through Knowledge and Wisdom, you will be able to inspire others. Jesus Christ also gave such an example: "You are the rock on which my church will be built." It is all part of a process. If you fall, do not give up, just get up and try again. Do not worry about minor detours; you can rejoin the main road. Everything is allowed, as long as you do not forget your main goal – your destination.

Remember that *Dvaraka* can be in your heart. That is the beauty of *Dvaraka*. Although the battle was won, Krishna decided not to get involved in further challenges. He decided to go to the ocean, asking the ocean to give Him land to build His Kingdom there, without asking for any help from the mainland. Everything started afresh, the Divine Architect was summoned, He was given the plan and in no time the whole city was ready. Krishna entered into the city with all the souls who wanted to be with Him physically, and the Divine *Lila* began, out of this world and away from the whole of humanity: the land of Krishna – the Island of *Dvaraka*.

Meanwhile there was Narada, the Cosmic Traveller, who was confused: "There are thousands there who love Krishna; how can He attend to them all?" Narada needed advice and decided to consult Lord Shiva in *Kailash*: "Oh *Mahadev*, do please tell me one thing, I am really confused: there are so many who love Krishna and are with Him in *Dvaraka* – how can He possibly attend to them all?" Shiva pondered a moment, then replied: "The best advice I can give you is to go to *Dvaraka* and find out for yourself. If I explained, you would not be completely satisfied. It may be best to go there in disguise, so that you will not be recognized."

So Narada – in disguise – returned to *Dvaraka*. He went from house to house to inspect. "Aha," he thought, "there is Krishna gardening with some *gopis*, tending the flowers. So that is where He is." In the second house however, he saw Krishna playing with the cows and several other *gopis*. The third house found Krishna cooking with yet another *gopi*. In that vein, many more houses showed Krishna engaged in some activity with more *gopis*. He did not find a single house without Krishna doing something. Poor Narada! Now he was even more confused. Going back to Shiva, he related what he saw. Shiva only smiled and said: "Do not try to figure it out, leave it at that for now. Just meditate – while your intellect cannot figure it out; meditation will help you understand the mystery."

This is only one of the stories of *Dvaraka*. There are many different narrations, but the focal point here is that, although you are living in *Kali Yuga*, and you live in the world – and the world is at its lowest consciousness today – you can create your own world. You have that possibility, but you have to be strong in your pursuit. You have to be clear, firm and focused like any disciple.

This reminds me of a story from the *Ramayana*. A *Guru* had one disciple. His name was Sutikshna. He was apprenticed at the young age of eighteen. The *Guru* saw some potential in him, so he allowed Sutikshna to serve him. *Guruji* and his new disciple were travelling in India from place to place by foot.

This little disciple was too young to take serious things

seriously. Thus they walked, and it became the disciple's duty to carry the deity or god, which in this case was a small Shiva lingam. The ritual required that every morning you bathe the "god," offer food, and do *puja* – every day. You treat it like a living God who is travelling with you. You offer *arati*, food, a bath and new clothes that you carry in a little shrine with you. That was the routine. One day, after the morning *puja* was complete, both *Guru* and disciple were relaxing. It was a hot day, and the relaxation under a Jamun tree was very pleasant. This tree bears a very delicious fruit, which is round and has a blue-black color, a little like plums, but with a different taste. As the young disciple was relaxing, one of these fruits fell and dropped right into his mouth. He tasted the fruit and found it most delicious. Naturally, he wanted more, but the fruit was very high up and he could not reach it. He pondered about this problem. The land around him was only plain earth, he could not find any stone, but he wanted the tasty fruit very much. He also could not climb: the trunk of the tree was very straight and smooth. Suddenly he remembered the Shiva lingam. Nice and solid! He said to himself, "I do not think 'god' would mind. Anyway, *Guruji* is sleeping. He will not notice." Then the disciple took the Shiva lingam, which is round and has a nice weight, and he threw it up into the tree. Success! Many fruits fell, lots of fruits, hundreds of fruits. The only problem was that "god" got stuck. "God" would not come down from the tree; maybe he decided to be there in the tree and relax. Well, the disciple's first concern was to eat and enjoy the fruit.

When he had eaten enough of the delicious Jamun, he thought of "god," still stuck up in the tree. Desperately he prayed: "Please God, come down." No matter how hard he tried, nothing happened. Meanwhile, it was time for *Guruji* to get up, and the disciple was worried sick: "What shall I say to *Guruji*?"

After all, he was a very young apprentice. He was terrified. While *Guruji* was preparing to get up, the disciple was panicking. He did not know what to do; the "god" just would not come down from the tree. So he decided: "Well, this Jamun fruit looks very similar to the "god" – same colour, same size. I will put it there instead. *Guruji* will not even notice." Everything seemed fine. *Guruji* got up, gave him some water and some refreshment, some Jamun actually, and everything was good.

The next morning, as ritual demanded giving a bath to "god," the "god" was installed on the silver plate and the *Guru* was pouring water... However, when he tried to give "god" a massage, to his dismay, he realized that the god's skin was peeling! He could not understand – is God not well today? How could the "god" transform into such a "something?" He was very worried until he examined the "god" carefully. To his surprise, he discovered that it was not his true "god," but a Jamun fruit.

This situation was food for thought, especially since *Guruji* noticed that his disciple was trying to hide from him. *Guruji* called, sternly: "Sutikshna! Come here! What have you done to my 'god?'" At first the disciple could not say anything. "Tell me the truth," demanded the *Guru*. Finally Sutikshna stammered and confessed what had happened. *Guruji* could not control his anger and told Sutikshna to get out of his sight. "Only when you get my 'god' back should you dare to come before me again!" The seriousness of the situation finally dawned on Sutikshna. He realized what a stupid thing he had done, and that his *Guru's* anger could not be reversed – that he was serious and had thrown him out of his presence. He also felt that he would never be able to come back, because how would he be able to find that "god?" He became very thoughtful and said: "Very well, I accept your command that I have to go away from you, but I promise you that not only will I bring your 'god' back, I will bring the Living God." With that, he left and went into meditation. Much time passed; an age passed while he was in meditation, invoking God and waiting for the Living God to appear.

It was during that time that Lord Rama had incarnated. Having to visit all His devotees and disciples, Sutikshna was also on his "list." Someone said to Sutikshna: "Lord Rama is coming to see you. Your meditation, your *tapasya*, is complete." Sutikshna tried to climb the tree to see if Rama was approaching, but he could not see anyone. After some time of climbing up and down the tree, he decided that this was a futile effort. Instead, he withdrew from all outside things and returned to his meditations to install Rama in his heart. Rama appeared at last, telling Sutikshna: "I am here. Open your eyes." Sutikshna said: "What guarantee do You give me? I may open my eyes and You are not there." Rama responded: "The guarantee is that your *tapasya* is complete – you have completed your task, your meditation. I know that you want to keep Me in your heart, but it would also be nice if you were to open your eyes and look at Me in front of you."

Sutikshna opened his eyes and saw the Living God Rama – the incarnation of Vishnu – standing there. Rama said: "Ask anything," and Sutikshna responded: "I have nothing to ask for myself. I have You in my heart, and I will have You and Your Energy forever. What more can I ask? However, I promised my *Guruji* to bring You to him; that I would like." Rama agreed and both set off to find *Guruji*. Eventually Sutikshna stood before *Guruji* and said: "I have done what I promised. Please forgive me for having been so childish and stupid." *Guruji* said: "Were it not for that 'stupidity and childishness,' the Living Rama would not be in front of me. I am grateful, Sutikshna."

The point is here to show what endeavor, determination and focus can do – that a young disciple, who had no idea about anything, can reach such a height is the real beauty of the story. Sutikshna was a simple disciple, basically a child with no concept but a pure heart. He was innocent and with a love for his *Guru* so immense that, even when separated from him, he built a statue of his Master and practiced *sadhana*.

Life is the most beautiful gift you have been given – your body, your mind and your senses are wonderful. You have the greatest tools, plus the spiritual guidance, to evolve. Many impossible tasks have been achieved and the very fact that you have a human life, that you have been given this opportunity of a human life as a doorway to the Ultimate Achievement of Enlightenment, should be the paramount reason to never give up striving to achieve that goal. Never mind if you have a mini-detour of life: always remember your aim and purpose and that the door to the *tirth* is open to you.

11

Striving for Wisdom

As we all know there is much beauty in the world but also ugliness. By nature the world is beautiful, but what humans have done and still do to the world can often be different – and destructive.

It seems that human *karma* is the most important factor in this. As mentioned many times before, you have collective as well as individual *karma*. Over the collective *karma* you have very little control since you are all part of the collective consciousness. For instance, a vast majority may make a collective decision, and although you may not like it, you are still part of it. However, where individual *karma* is concerned, it is your responsibility how you manage your time, your activities and your resources. Although you are part of the greater consciousness, you can still determine decisions on how to handle your own life and how to deal with your *karmic* duty.

Spiritual Knowledge is supposed to make you wiser; you may have been practicing all sorts of techniques or methods over the years and may have been listening to many spiritual discourses. Armed with such Knowledge, you are supposed to be advancing and becoming clearer. Then an interesting question arises: what is Wisdom and who actually is wise?

In India, if someone is wise, he or she is considered

Paramahansa – the Supreme Swan. You may ask: why a swan? According to legend, swans have the capability of perfect discrimination. For instance, it is said that if one mixes water and milk and offer these to a swan, the swan will take the milk and leave the rest. That discriminating quality of the swan illustrates Wisdom – to know what to take and what to leave. Thus, when someone is given the title of "Swan," it would imply that that person has acquired the quality of profound discrimination, as in the title *"Srimad Paramahansa."*

The manifestation of Wisdom is that when something is presented to you, you would know instinctively and intuitively what is right and what is wrong. Take the example of someone offering you a special tea: you may know instantly what kind of tea this is, what the ingredients are and whether it is healthy and good for you – or not. Birds, for instance, have a natural way of selecting what is good for them: you may give them a mixture of grains, stones and all kinds of other things, but they will know exactly what grain to choose and leave all the rest. Now, this is not an indication of "bird wisdom," but it underlines the principle of discrimination in all areas of life. It is up to you to discover what is good for you and what is not.

Then what is a "wise person?" The wise person knows the world and understands it. He cannot be fooled by superficial and misleading information. If you follow the Path of Wisdom, you are supposed to become more intuitive. The problem with the average person is that he/she is defeated in the first round of the battle for Wisdom. Each round becomes more difficult and challenging.

When you are presented with some mixture of negativity and positivity, you often get confused, maybe distressed. There is a proverb in India: "If someone tells you that some of your possessions had been stolen, you do not run after the supposed robber, until you have checked your belongings." It is good for you to follow the Path of Wisdom, thereby achieving the stability of a rock. Any time someone makes an unpleasant comment and you become disturbed – that is not Wisdom. The story of Buddha and his disciple Ananda illustrates this principle perfectly. We have mentioned the example many times before.[1]

Mahatma Gandhi followed the Path of *ahinsa* and implemented this in daily life. Consider the demeanor of an elephant who pays no attention to the barking dogs following him. An elephant knows his own strength and is not bothered by the irate dogs. If you pay attention to the noise going on around you, it means you have not learned to discriminate. Otherwise, why would you get disturbed if someone wants to pollute your mind? Do not fall into the trap of someone's attempts to disturb you with all kinds of negative nonsense – either orally or in writing. Especially nowadays, emails are an easy vehicle to convey almost anything, including misleading, nasty and at times vicious attacks. As long as you allow yourself to be affected, disturbed, upset and insecure by such attacks, Wisdom is still far from you.

Wisdom comes out of spontaneous intuition. Speaking about mail and email, you may receive letters or emails and some of them may be extremely hurtful. Consider receiving a letter or email from someone you know who does not have good intentions. Is it a fair estimation that by just a quick glance at the sender you might get a very good idea of the "tone" of

---

1 See the following publications:
  Exploring Within
  So You Shall Know the Truth
  Practical Wisdom

the message? You know – and if you know that the message is likely to be spiteful, mean or nasty, why would you bother to read it all, thereby polluting your mind? If you do read it, you are allowing that negative thought to access your mind, thereby entering your system, just as when you eat spoilt food that makes you feel unwell. Any kind of toxic thought resembles drinking poison – the substance has already entered your bloodstream and you have lost control. Then you are left with the task of trying to clear the pollution – sometimes it can linger for a long time. Wisdom will tell you instantly what is right and what is wrong; there is no need to ask anyone. You just know.

The mystic saint and poet Saint Mira (Mirabai) of the early 16th century was born into a royal family. While still a young girl she fell in love with Krishna. Those around her, family and courtiers, wanted her to attend to her royal duties. All kinds of complaints were raised against her by those who did not want her to follow the Divine Path. There is a saying that love is blind – spiritual longing for Enlightenment is similarly blind. Just as human love empowers you to forget other aspects, you can imagine how much this is magnified in the spiritual Search. When you are blinded by love, then it does not matter if the whole world is against you. That is the strength of love; let all and everything become your enemy, it matters not. You simply do not care. Nothing can touch or affect you in realizing your objective.

One Master received a new and very eager disciple who claimed: "Oh Master, I am now Your number one disciple. I have studied for twelve years; I have studied the *Vedanta*, logic and many more disciplines. I have studied these things thoroughly for twelve years. Now I am qualified to take over Your ashram and run it for You. So, please hand it all over to me."

Master thought for a while and replied: "You may have studied for twelve years but there is one aspect you have not learned yet."

"Oh? What is that my Master?"

"That I cannot tell you – if you have not realized what it is you still need to learn. However, I will send you to my Friend's ashram and He will teach you."

The impatient disciple somewhat reluctantly accepted the Master's decision and went on his way to the other Master:

"My *Guru* has sent me to you to learn something very important which apparently I have missed. I do not know what it is that I have overlooked after all my studies for so many years; please teach me."

The Master looked at him for a while, then He picked up a broom that was standing nearby and gave it to him:

"Here you are, take this broom and sweep the ashram."

Our keen disciple was somewhat confounded. This was the lowliest job. After all, had he not learned everything in those twelve years? It was a hard lesson to learn for the enthusiastic aspirant.

Humility is very important in the spiritual life; without humility nothing will work. Without humility you cannot enter the spiritual gate. On one hand, it is easy to know everything; on the other hand, it is very difficult when you do not know what you need to know. In hindsight, you may realize that you could have done many things differently and better. The real Wisdom is to know instantly what is right and what is not – and to implement that. It is for you to strive for this instant recognition, to see the Truth for what Truth is without any distortions. You alone have to experience the Truth. Whenever someone else tries to make you see from his or her view, it does not make it your own view, your own experience. How can you know the Truth, the Wisdom, by viewing it through the mind of another?

Your view and understanding are yours alone. Your heart is your heart. Ask your heart. Why would you ask another about how you feel or experience? Whenever you ask your true heart, you will receive a true answer. How is it that you ignore your own instinct and the voice of your own heart and listen to the misleading or misrepresenting and misguiding feedback from others instead?

That is the basic idea of developing the skill of discrimination: to listen and pay attention to your own instincts and inner voice. This will bring refinement to your senses. It will improve your sense of taste by being able to separate different ingredients of a meal. It will enhance your sense of hearing by defining different sounds, like listening to an orchestra and singling out the different instruments. In nature, you can single out the rustling of leaves in the breeze, maybe the chirping or song of birds, each with their individual calls, or maybe a small brook bubbling over the rocks. It is an interesting experience to listen carefully and to separate the sounds of the total "symphony." The same principle applies to the sense of smell, like being able to discriminate among different flowers or the sense of vision to recognize beauty.

There is no limit how far you can develop your mind and your faculties. In fact, you have two minds really: one which is polluted by daily disturbances; the other one which is clean and clear. The battle between those two is being waged daily. If we reflect and examine each faculty within our system, we can see how intricate their interaction is.

Once again: what makes you wise? Wisdom comes from within and when you open yourself. Yet there are so many outer forces to disturb and to muddy the inner view that clarity of vision is often difficult. Why is it that people have a tendency to wish for confirmation of their own understanding from someone else? The need for confirmation from outside forces is simply a lack of personal development.

The day you become fulfilled, you do not need to ask anyone; you need no confirmation of who and what you are. This is what you are striving toward. You are working toward that goal where you do not depend on anything. Then everything will be spontaneous and intuitive; you do things instinctively and everything just flows. It is on that level where High Beings operate, and whatever they do will always be right and never wrong or harmful. Their lives become models by themselves. They function on a much higher level of consciousness.

Striving for Knowledge and Wisdom continues in the battle between the positive and the negative, between light and dark. Try not to be caught up in this battle. Almost everybody goes through the battle of life. It is up to you to sort out your own battle. You do your bit and follow your Path, never mind anyone else.

In the *Bhagavad Gita*, Krishna reminds Arjuna: "Your action is not a question of choice; you do not have a choice whether to fight or not. You have to fight. You have to act. Everybody has to act. Your whole life is one of action, whether you like it or not; you cannot remain inactive."

The question is: do you want to do good work or bad? There is no escape from action in this life; you cannot live without action, without doing. It is the law of life. The choice you have is that of doing creative, positive and enlightening work, or indulging in non-creative negative activity. You have absolute freedom to make your choice – and take the consequences. Those who choose the Path of Light and positivity will be rewarded accordingly; and those who choose the path of darkness and negativity will only create conflict for themselves – unfortunately also for those who are involved with them.

Negativity can become a habit or way of life. Is this Life? What kind of life is this for some negative person to spend an entire lifespan in conflict and hate, to have a whole lifetime dedicated to causing harm and destruction? That kind of life portrays the real tragedy of the human being in the world. One can only hope that at some time during such a miserable life, some ray of light and sanity may penetrate and let such person realize his/her absurdity and waste and to make some positive changes.

On the other hand, you can maintain focus on that which is important for your ongoing striving for your development and growth – without taking stock of what everyone else is doing. Your life will be simpler and much more enjoyable and Wisdom may dawn.

12

For the Sake of Communication

Language is a means of communication, a mode of expression for the purpose of understanding. But the language of the Divine requires special understanding. To be able to communicate with the Divine and with those who have known the Divine – those who have reached the highest level of consciousness – is not an ordinary ability. You must uplift yourself in order to communicate.

The instinct for spiritual communication is inherent within everyone. When this unconscious urge becomes a conscious desire and need, Grace will manifest in physical form to communicate with the human being on the human level.

Such a High Being as a Satguru may appear so human that you may be confused, wondering, sometimes even doubting: how can this be, that this Enlightened Being can act like this, behave in such human manner? You cannot stand the Energy, the intensity of His Play, His Lila.

Grace becomes human so that the human being should know Divine Glory – and the state of Divine Consciousness. Human imagination can and will indulge in anything, yet the state of Highest Consciousness cannot be achieved by imagination. Imagination will not permit you to experience absolute bliss, peace and love. However, it has been said that what we love we shall grow to resemble.

Consider the Teachings and achievements of Realized Beings – Jesus, Guru Nanak, Lord Mahavir and many more – one can easily see how much they inspire people to serve, to devote, to dedicate and to love each other, and to radiate that Energy.

Devotion, dedication and love can cleanse your negative karma. Visualize the water of a lake: it may appear calm and clear during fair weather periods. Yet as soon as a storm springs up, mud and dirt from the bottom of the lake can turn the water so cloudy that the previously clear view will be completely obstructed – and your view will be just as muddy. Likewise, unless the "mud" of the mind is removed by steady devotion and selfless action, love, faith and trust, you will always be subjected to confusion and doubt every time "the wind springs up." This is the cleansing process to purify your heart, mind and intellect so that your view may become clear. Only then will you be able to see any situation with such clarity that you will know exactly how to act.

Since the mind is under the influence of the three *gunas* – *satva*, the pure and positive; *rajas*, the active and excitable; and *tamas*, the negative and inert – it will waver constantly. You cannot just run away from your responsibilities by announcing that you do not "feel" like doing something or the other. Try to analyze your feelings. The wavering mind, so easily influenced by desire, appearances or gossip, is unreliable and can be a veritable "snake pit" of wriggling and writhing negativities and fantasies. Then the question arises: do you follow all the impulses your mind creates – it may even wish to kill? Of course not. You think about it and then you take refuge in the Higher Teachings. You cannot trust your mind and therefore you cannot give importance to whatever your mind, or someone else's mind, concocts. You need to develop healthy discrimination – *viveka* – which is an attribute of the purified intellect. *Viveka* is based on your Higher Self, and it is never wrong.

A stanza from the *Kathopanishad* states: "Those who live in *samsara* are in the midst of ignorance and darkness. They have neither right understanding nor discrimination. They are held and bound by one-thousand-and-one ties of expectations. They are entangled in one-thousand-and-one meshes of attachments for children, wife, wealth and property."

Ties of attachments and expectations are imaginary ones. You have tied yourself to things which will pass away, which do not last. Rather, focus instead on discovering your real tie, your relationship with the Eternal, with God or *Satguru*. The relationship between the *Satguru* and disciple, between God and the soul, is so profound and deep that it cannot be separated. The *Satguru* will incarnate in order to help you uplift and to make you complete. Yet He will be very careful who He accepts as disciple. He will wait until He considers the disciple ready for, and worthy of, initiation; that the disciple is capable of fulfilling the vow taken during initiation. Such vow represents a total commitment for both *Satguru* and disciple – a sacred spiritual contract which is never to be taken lightly. It is the ultimate and final commitment.

It is a common mistake to think that the *Satguru* will have to come and liberate the disciple, once initiated, irrespective of the disciple's lifestyle, indulgencies and negativities. This is not so. It is true that the *Satguru* will never break the contract. However if the disciple violates his promise and, ignoring the vow, slips back into his old unhealthy thoughts and habits, the *Satguru* will cease to be bound by the contract.

It is a sad truth that the human being does not appreciate that which is given easily. It seems that only that which is gained after much hard work and hardship will truly be appreciated. It is the same with Knowledge. The profound Knowledge given by the *Satguru* is not easily understood. When He states: "Whatever you are, I am. I recognize you as Me," He means that He recognizes each individual as His own *Atman*. This demands a profound ability to truly understand, to communicate and to express. A popular Indian *Bhajan* conveys this truth beautifully: "*Hei Rama Mujhama, Mai Rame Mehu*," meaning: "I am in God, the Absolute, and He is in Me."

Everyone has the instinct of self-preservation, a reflection of the importance of the *Atman* and its expression. It is unfortunate that the distorted ego has laid claim to it. You are the most important thing, but you must find out what that YOU is. For as long as you are caught in *Maya*, illusion, it prevents you from recognizing this Truth. Unable to rid yourself of the sense of duality, you are entangled in the same old nets of attachments: my family, my house, my friend, my society, my profession. I, me and mine!

The human being's concept of "I" and "me" illustrates the basis of all suffering and trouble. You do not see the Mystery and the Truth. You may have studied all the scriptures, yet all the book knowledge in the world will not give you Enlightenment. Divine Knowledge can only manifest when you have prepared yourself. If you follow the instructions of your Spiritual Preceptor faithfully, carry out your *sadhana* diligently, one day – maybe quite suddenly – you will know all. In the meantime do not plan. Instead, try to fit into the *plan* which has been made for you already. Unfortunately, human nature has plans and ideas of its own which are contradictory to the Divine Plan and thus doomed to fail miserably.

On the way towards communication with the Highest, there are different stages of consciousness. You will have to undergo the "death" of all the accumulated negativity and conditioning – attachments to places, people and habits – in order to be born into a higher state of consciousness. When spiritual birth takes place, everything becomes new. You will have discovered the permanent relationship which transcends everything and which lasts eternally. The relationship with the *Satguru* is absolutely indestructible. Once this great insight has been attained, all your problems will cease.

The idea is to make use of everything. Do not allow yourself to become deluded and confused, undermined by unstable emotions and wavering mind. It is important to strive constantly for stability and to have a total commitment to the *Satguru*. Say to yourself: "From this day I will give top priority to the greatest cause in my life. Everything else will follow accordingly." With such a resolution firmly established in your daily life, nothing and no one should prevent you from your birthright: Communication with the Infinite.

13

Perception of Pain and Suffering

Physical suffering is also a part of life and part of the Teaching, reminding us not to take anything for granted. Many times you forget that life is a gift and a privilege, not a right. There is a difference between right and privilege; you may consider things to be your right, demanding that it should be like this or like that. That is not the case.

In the spiritual world there is no such thing as "right." The only thing you have is what is in your power to do. When any kind of trouble comes into your life, it is a reminder that life is a precious gift and to be appreciated without complaints. Instead be grateful and treasure what you have and try to do the best both mentally and physically. That will help to enrich your future. Consider any kind of trouble in your life as a reminder and a warning. Attempting to assert your rights will not help. Instead, appreciate daily how fortunate and privileged you are.

Tulsidas said: "In this life I have been given the opportunity to live to the fullest." You too have been given the beautiful world, an excellent body, and a superb mind with all its faculties – you have no reason to complain. You have every reason to be happy, appreciative and grateful.

Some of the spiritual seekers in the Himalayas have renounced the world and deliberately gone through many hardships of life; they live without food and shelter and they may expose themselves to every imaginable danger and extreme circumstances. In fact, they are making a statement to the world: nothing can make me unhappy – I will be happy by my own True Nature.

Sometimes Great Masters will subject themselves to the extremes of trouble by actually making a statement to nature (or *Maya*): "What trouble can you give Me when I have already adopted all your extremes?" This is a way of addressing those forces which are trying to create trouble for you: "Come on, you have tried all this before, you cannot make me unhappy."

Moreover, sometimes aspirants, seekers (or *sadhus*) endure extreme conditions deliberately to overcome fears, whatever they may be. How do you accept and how do you handle both physical pain and emotional pain? Every pain that comes to you has a message.

It is also interesting that when you are not well, other faculties become more pronounced and supportive, strong and powerful. Not all the faculties let you down; some are there to help you to overcome the suffering. Often, when pain manifests, it is followed by a greater energy boom. Normally one would expect more pain to follow, but somehow there is a positive energy influx. This is another phenomenon of physical or mental suffering, that behind every suffering a greater strength will manifest. You are determined to defeat that pain and suffering, and you are saying: "You cannot pull me down. You are not my master. You are my subject." That kind of strength and energy comes from the *Atma*, your Self. That is why *Atma* is described as the most powerful element in the whole system.

It is said in *Vedanta*: "Those who do not have the strength will not realize *Atma*, and those who are tired, lazy and self-pitying are not worthy of *Atma*."

The *Upanishads* state: "One who has the strength, one who is brave, one who has a burning desire, only he can realize the *Atma*."

Of course the scriptures do not speak of physical strength; it has nothing to do with your size or your general well-being. Pain and suffering are very subjective – when you hurt yourself and you are distracted by something more striking, you may be totally unaware of the pain. You will only be aware of the injury and its associated pain when you relax. That kind of subjectivity is also dependent on your inherent attitude – whether you like to do something or not. Such likes or dislikes actually defeat the whole subject. According to your personal priorities, pain and suffering may not even exist. Give this concept some thought.

It is a common factor that especially older people will always talk about doctors and hospitals. It is not helpful to dwell on disease and pain. It is also not helpful to commiserate with someone unwell or in pain by telling them that you had the same problem. However, if you go to someone and you are there to help – to be part of a support system – that is very beneficial. Many people, especially when older and not well, may have a sense of abandonment, feeling lonely and forgotten, feeling that nobody cares. That is the worst feeling in any stage of life, but particularly when you are older. When you are assured that you have support and help, even if you do not actually need this, it is still a great strength. You may have family and friends around, but essentially it is the attitude of the caregiver that is the most important feature for the person who is suffering and in that person's ongoing recovery.

Another example is that of those women who are horrifically abused, beaten and tortured by their living companion. One single gesture of kindness from the abuser will make them forget and forgive all the suffering they have endured. That is truly phenomenal. Then where is the pain of the beating, the suffering of kicking and the ongoing verbal, psychological and physical abuse – when with a perceived small kindness all is forgotten?

Once again it proves the subjectivity of pain and suffering. Physical and mental pain is totally relative in a person's life. In the final analysis, pain is a perception of your mind. It is all a question of how you receive and perceive things. The whole system is so interesting that when you go into each area of your life, you will find a fascinating scene with many different vistas to contemplate.

14

Kriya Yoga

Yoga has been explained in many ways and *yoga* has many different meanings and applications. *Yoga* encompasses physical, mental and spiritual disciplines. The final goal of any type of *yoga* is the attainment of union and completeness with the task one has undertaken to achieve the Final Reality.

Through the system of *yoga*, not only is the practitioner helped spiritually, but also there are physical and material benefits. These benefits enable and facilitate an increase in physical health and strength, as well as training the mind and intellect. The practice of *yoga* will also improve the practitioner's capacity to contemplate and to distinguish right from wrong, eventually leading to an increased mastery of oneself – body, mind and intellect.

Kriya yoga has two forms of manifestation: one is gross and the other is subtle. The particular term *"kriya"* has to be understood at the onset. Any performance of body and mind can classify as *kriya*. *Maya* is the root of the main principle and *kriya* is its manifestation. One could also say that *kriya* is one of the vehicles of *Maya*.

Actually, there is no such thing as *"kriya yoga;"* this term has been created for the West as a combination of various practices. In fact, *kriya yoga* is related to six cleansing processes

– *sat karma* in *Sanskrit* – as set out in Patanjali's *sutras*. It is the beauty of the *Sanskrit* language that, if you know the language, you can shape it to create your own term indicating your particular meaning, association and context. Although this is possible in many other languages to some degree, it is the richness of the *Sanskrit* language – with the range of its roots – which makes it especially suitable.

As indicated, there is no traditional term as *"kriya yoga,"* but people have become familiar with it. There are certain techniques which are related to the body as well as to the mind. These techniques are very interesting as well as stimulating. Once you are engaged in those activities or techniques, you can continue to practice them for many months, even years, in order to complete the *kriya yoga* – similar to a *tapasya*. Even with *tapasya*, you could continue the entire life and yet never complete; like standing in freezing water for an extended length of time, or conversely, sitting within a blazing hot circle of roaring flames, or sleeping on thorny beds, and many more extremes.

While these are gross physical practices, there are also subtler or less extreme practices such as changing some ingrained habits. Examples are the avoidance of certain foods or drinks one has become attached to. Countless changes can be adopted based on the individual's attachment to certain habits. The main point of this kind of *kriya* or *tapasya* is to break the conditions of body and mind; that neither body nor mind depend on a particular habit, substance or particular way of living. In this way, body and mind are trained to accept, as well as to adjust and accommodate to, changes in all situations.

This is the meaning of *tapasya*, *kriya* and *sadhana*. Through these various exercises, one strengthens both body and mind in such a way that one is ready to act according to the need of the time or the force of circumstances, rather than maintaining the old habits and reactions. Through Knowledge, one can overcome this; the practices will help to give a purpose and a goal. The main purpose of going through such *sadhana* and *kriya* is to overcome the blockages and the obstacles which you have created in body and mind.

Aspire to let your body and mind become ready to act and react to the force of circumstances and the demand of the moment. When you are forced into a situation you can respond automatically, so genuinely that the very situation does not exist or disappears in no time. For instance, you may be forced into an extreme event or situation such as a serious incident or accident that causes mass panic, a situation of high anxiety. The idea is to be able to maintain your individuality and not lose your identity when the collective negative psychology and force is all around you.

Of course, if there is a positive force and you are a positive person, then you will be able to adjust yourself accordingly. But if you are a positive force and the negative force surrounding you is much stronger, then the question arises: How much of your positive force are you prepared to give up, accepting the negative? All those things are there to test and try you. The idea is to make yourself perfect and to act and react appropriately, according to the need of the time and situation.

There are many things that can bring about a change in belief. Some people have certain beliefs, some do not; others again are made to believe, or not to believe, certain ideas or ideologies. All these are merely conditions of mind that have been formed. But if you have trained yourself, you are ready. Compare this to a soldier's training before he enters a war: training involves very hard physical and mental preparation and discipline. He will be exposed to countless different situations that he may come across in battle and that he must master in order to survive or prevent injury. Certain things are to be given up whereas others are to be accepted, resulting in strong discipline. When the time comes, in a crisis, this training can save the soldier's life.

You can apply certain disciplines to yourself: making affirmations to achieve more positive conduct. There are many more disciplines to go through. After you have gone through all of this, mastered many physical and mental disciplines, one phase of your training has been completed. When it comes to the test of performance in real action, you will see how you handle yourself.

This is *kriya yoga* or *tapasya*, the very basis of which is rooted in your thinking. In Jainism, training is very similar yet more on a direct and physical basis. You may be put in certain situations – both physical and psychological – and your reaction should be no more than the actual event warrants. For instance, someone may hit you and see if you become angry, or, if water is thrown on you, an appropriate reaction is to shake it off and to dry yourself without feeling anger at the person who performed the act. Someone may make an unpleasant comment to see if your ego is touched and whether you react. The point is to see whether you can apply the right thinking, right Knowledge, intuition and Wisdom you have been taught without emotional reaction. You may see something you like and since you lack that particular thing, you may become envious or jealous – without applying the Knowledge. Ask yourself: What reason do I have to be envious or jealous? This may have been the way you reacted in the past, but can you overcome the past, live in the present and make the future bright?

Kriya yoga is based on similar principles, although on a more technical and physical basis, accepting certain deprivation and controlling the senses to induce a kind of meditative state. Those *kriya* can help, but if you are not prepared by the Knowledge and the Wisdom and awareness of the background, then the benefit of all your efforts is considerably reduced. Only when you have the Knowledge and Wisdom behind any kind of *tapasya* or *kriya* will the result be more fulfilling and vital. Indeed, every practice or act should lead to more evolution and overall understanding.

In Eastern philosophy, a *kriya* is much more associated with ritual to please and petition a deity. While Westerners may be interested, the psychology in the West is different and such practice usually presents difficulties for the Western mind. Eastern philosophy is familiar with the inherent totality of the individual being and although nothing is suppressed, one is aware of the very root of one's being. This is not the case in Western psychology; to repeat any action over and over for its own sake does not provide spiritual progress, except for perhaps gaining some discipline. How long can you continue with that exercise? The danger is also that whatever you might "see" in your practices, you also become part of that, and if you lose your identity in the process, that means you become subject to that "thing." For instance, if you were to join the society of cheating, you would become a cheat. Thereafter, your power to maintain your individual identity and to object to any of their practices or beliefs is gone. You have no control and you have lost the ability to move forward and onward.

This is what happens: if you lose your individuality,

you become subject to whatever surrounds you. This may be television, food, certain activities such as gossip, or a particular group of people. Once this attachment has been formed within you, it is very difficult to overcome, because the demand for continuation of these behaviors and habits within you is great.

Take the example of a spy. He knows what he is and who he is working for, yet he will go to a meeting where he will be introduced to all the political and social dignitaries and he behaves quite naturally. Nobody knows that he is a spy with a different agenda. He never loses his identity and that awareness is constantly part of him. He knows his job and does not lose his character and his identity as a spy. The moment he loses his individuality, he will not be able to continue his work as a spy.

That is the kind of identity to strive for: to know that you are not this, not that and not the other, even though you have to live within the confines of *Maya*. Therefore it is your *tapasya*, your *kriya*, to make yourself so strong and to further your goal to the extent that nothing else can touch you, although you can touch everything. You are the one to enjoy, not that "thing" – that person, idea or ideology – that is enjoying you. You make the decision to do something you choose, instead of being forced to do something you do not want. That is the kind of control that can evolve through *kriya*.

Nowadays there are countless "courses" in schools or colleges – especially in the West – that may offer you instant or fast-track *moksha*. That is no more than senseless advertising. Of course there are some courses that might help to increase your knowledge and techniques, like courses in *hatha yoga* instruction or relaxation and many more. All of these can be very helpful, but they do not assist you to attain Higher Growth. If you think that going through therapy, courses and seminars you will make yourself grow, forget that. That is not the way; it is only a limited means to achieve a temporary feel-good factor. For the purpose of attaining Higher Growth, you have to work very hard on yourself, implementing the Teachings. For that, you need individual guidance and attention. Even then, you need to make a sincere effort to overcome challenges. Only once your mind is purified can you see things clearly in the bright Light.

Actually, there are some exercises, some *kriya*, that are beneficial. For instance, "closing the nine gates" is one of the *kriya*, or "blacking out the mind," or "listening to the Inner Sound," the *Anahat*, that is going on within you. These are not things you can just practice once or twice. It is a pity that people hear about such disciplines and get very excited, wanting to go ahead without knowing whether they are capable of doing these practices or not. Some just want to go through the motions to perform these advanced *kriya* mechanically. Yes, it can be done mechanically, but there will be very limited benefit. Any worthwhile *kriya* has to be taught by an expert and the student has to apply him/herself thoroughly and with dedication. Simply jumping around from one exercise to another is useless.

For example, just reading an interesting article will create more conditioning of the mind; it can often cause an obsession with the particular idea or exercise. The problem is that once conditioned in this way, you do not want to know anything else but what you have read. Instead, try thinking about what you have read and consider that this is just one view. This will leave you open to other possibilities. One thought, one belief, can dominate you so thoroughly that it can take you over to the extent that you are not able to overcome this hurdle. First of all, find out what "belief" actually is. What are your beliefs? The dictionary lists "belief" as: *"an opinion or a conviction – confidence in the truth or existence of something not immediately susceptible to rigorous proof."*

You may say that you believe in the sun and the moon and the ocean and the trees. Can you say that although I believe in the sun, I reject the moon – I believe in the wind, but I reject the fire? They are all part of creation. Can you say that I believe in my mother but not in my father or in my brother and not in my sister? They are all part of your family, all aspects of the same unit, and whether you like one better than the other has nothing to do with that.

You need to carefully examine what belief actually is. Different religions, for instance, just focus on one aspect, accepting one deity and rejecting all others. Although religion may profess to disseminate higher principles, it is often limited by the understanding and conduct of the followers.

There is no doubt that there is only One Truth. The greatest *mantra*, *Purna Mantra*, perfectly outlines the fact that nothing is incomplete:

Purnamadah Purnamidam;
Purnat Purnamudachyate
Purnasya Purnamadaya;
Purnamevavashisyate,

<u>translated from the *Sanskrit*:</u>

This is whole;
That is whole;
Taking away whole from whole,
Whole still remains whole.

Cultures which encompass many "gods" are often

misunderstood. Since the *many* are actually only aspects of the *One* – the many manifestations of the One Absolute, often referred to as God – these many manifestations actually allow people to relate to a deity according to individual temperament or inclination.

This approach can be positive, since it offers complete freedom to relate to that aspect of the Divine which is most dear and most sacred to the individual. Since everyone has different inclinations, different talents, and different emotional make-ups, they can choose the aspect that they identify with. At the same time, you do not reject all the other manifestations, knowing that they are all aspects of the same God. It is actually a very logical concept; to understand that although the Divine is One, the manifestations of the One are many – many forms, symbols and entities like the sun, moon, mountains, rivers and so on.

It is a great freedom to accept these many manifestations and to be given the choice to grow through them. After all, you do not know the Final Mystery and therefore it is wise to grow through a positive aspect. For the average human being to claim Knowledge of that Mystery is like an ant claiming knowledge of an elephant. This is an apt comparison.

Instead, accept that Teaching which is based on Higher Growth and do not reject anything else; just do not give much attention to negative feedback. Rejection is not wise: accept what is positive and grow through it. It is enough to ignore, and far better than to hate, for hate will reflect back onto you and it can take you over.

In general, people do not think about what they are being taught; mostly they are just floating in the current of the prevailing wave, without any awareness whatsoever. Take the example of television: one person with his or her particular opinion or "belief" can change the opinion of millions. If, however, you have a discerning consciousness, then you can apply the right sense as an individual. Even then people will not necessarily support you, although in time, they may come to respect you when they see that you are much more developed in thought and performance than they are.

Suppose you listen to a meaningful thought and then just forget it. What is the use of that? However, when listening to the thought, followed by contemplation and implementation, then belief or non-belief does not even occur. It is no longer an opinion. Instead, it has become a tool that can be tested to see how it works and it can be put into practice. That is the way it should be.

It is a tragedy that thoughtful examination of any Teaching is rarely implemented; many just listen and then they forget; worse it can be considered a form of entertainment by some. It has become a way to please the mind and senses; consequently, if you find it pleasing, you participate and if not, you just walk away. That is the prevailing psychology of the mind.

Only if you can make an effort to analyze, contemplate and implement the Teaching given, will you derive a much more substantial benefit. That contemplation – analysis and implementation – is the kind of *kriya* that is recommended for all.

15

Choices of Meditation

Whenever you meditate, many different types of energy are being released. Consider the subconscious during sleep; in the subconscious state, many impressions are being discharged and measured as dreams. Similarly, in meditation, all kinds of suppressed energy will be released.

The goal is to let all those energies which are not helpful pass and rather focus on those which are supportive. Obviously, if you concentrate on the wrong thoughts your meditation will be unsettled with the release of energies you may not care for. But if you can ignore those negative impulses and pay attention to the positive and helpful energies, then you are on the right track.

Normally, during the day, when you are busy with all kinds of thoughts, maybe sitting and talking to someone, or eating, or walking or engaged in many other activities, you do not have the chance to have concentrated focus. In meditation, when you suspend physical activities, mental activities will increase automatically. If you dwell on negative impulses or thoughts during meditation, of course you will be disturbed. This is not a meditative state. Instead, you have to observe and check these influences and keep neutralizing them. This way, you are not affected by those thoughts which are there to unsettle you. At night, however, when you are relaxed, it may be easier to tune out the constant chatter of the mind and you can slide into meditation. The meditative state is a very special state of your mind. To achieve this may require a little effort at first, but after some time you will automatically slide into effortless meditation. The first phase of meditation is not to identify with anything, just letting things pass, considering yourself a witness of all the thoughts drifting through your mind.

When you make an effort to meditate, you will create a different and separate state of mind and separate energies are released. Then you have the opportunity to uplift yourself and to direct the focus more deeply into yourself. Although there are many different types of meditation, a basic meditation is where you focus on something. By way of example: the meditation of the Buddhist monk is to try and empty the mind. Buddhist monks walk very slowly; it can happen that in one hour they may only walk 100 meters. That is their meditative walk: no hurry, no destination, no appointment. It is recommended to practice this kind of meditation, especially during times of stress. Walk very slowly, try to empty your mind and discard any thoughts that come: "not this, and not this, and not this..." One of the most effective and fulfilling ways is to meditate on the play of your life, like replaying the positive aspects of your life. Another form of meditation is more personal: when you are traveling to see your *Satguru* or Teacher, your focus is entirely on that Being and all else is tuned out.

In Hinduism, the predominant focus of meditation is on the *Ishta*, that deity who to the individual is the personification of the Highest – be that Rama, Krishna, Kali, or any aspect which is most meaningful to the worshipper. He or she would visualize that deity, presenting a flower, light, maybe some juice and special food. That is the predominant way of meditation in Hinduism. The most popular meditation in India is that the disciple, devotee or student will make an offering to the *Satguru* of flowers and fruit. This kind of meditation does not involve much thought since the disciple is actually participating.

Of course meditation on the *Satguru* is always popular because you interact personally with Him; you can visualize or replay the Knowledge He has given to you or you can also offer flowers, light, and special food, like *kheer* – rice pudding. It is said that when the Buddha was in deep meditation, a beautiful young woman came every day, bringing fresh *kheer* and waiting for Him to wake up. Of course while the Master was not eating, neither did she, fasting for a long time. That became her meditation: her entire focus and attention was on this Being sitting under the Banyan tree. When finally the Master did awaken, this young woman was there with her offering of rice pudding. It became the Buddha's first food – and she became the first disciple.

Meditation is the creation of a newer state of mind. You have a wakeful consciousness, a sleep consciousness, and when you meditate you create a meditation consciousness. That is your effort and your work. It will regulate your senses, your mind and your self. There is a meditation for beginners, a somewhat more advanced meditation, and a very advanced meditation, finally followed by *samadhi*, the highest form of meditation. *Samadhi* of course is not for everyone. Only the Highest *Yogi* can achieve that. Once you are in *samadhi*, it can happen that days, months and even years pass. The question is: can your physical body survive while all its activities have been suspended? For the state of *samadhi*, the body has to be trained and prepared; it is a suspension of all outer life. This is the very highest form of meditation. This is why *yogis* may use the alchemical process of *rasayana*.

Samadhi is like a "beyond death" experience – an out-of-body experience. Since the body is not active, the senses and organs are suspended in a form of hibernation. In some way, this is not so unusual and certainly not impossible. Bears and many other animals do it automatically. For instance, a bear goes into hibernation in winter for up to six months while snakes go underground in the hot summer period. It is not a fantasy but a reality that bodily functions can be suspended for a prolonged time.

However, for a human body to survive in this state, you will have to be a great *yogi*, and you will have to know how to prepare and protect your body, your senses and your organs and keep them healthy while in this state. You know that when you awaken from a sound eight-hour sleep, your body may be rather stiff and inflexible and it will take a little while to regain normal function and activities. Now compare this to going into *samadhi* for six months or more. Your body would have had to have undergone meticulous training in order to adjust. Without such training, one can consider a person in a coma whose ongoing survival relies on external support.

Therefore, do not be concerned about *samadhi*; leave this to the evolved *yogis*. For the time being, meditation is enough. This is why I recommend doing meditation before sleep and after sleep. Meditation before sleep, even recalling and contemplating all the beautiful things in your life, can be meditation and it will carry good thoughts into your sleep. You may choose whatever meditation is the easiest for you. In this way the body becomes more relaxed, different functions are neutralized, and sleep and dream quality is much better.

On awakening, when you meditate for half an hour,

the positive trend from the previous night's meditation and the good sleep will be continued. This will also prevent you from awakening with a sensation of depression which is a serious hindrance to your well-being and should be avoided. When you awaken and you are happy, the world looks good to you. That is the kind of meditation which grounds you.

These are the many choices of meditation. A personal teacher is very important to guide you from one stage to the next.

16

Meditation and *Maya*

Many times we have discussed different styles of meditation, from gently focusing on the movement of your breath, to clearing your mind and many other others. There is one type of meditation which is the easiest to follow: you simply focus on your *Ishta*, your preferred deity or concept image of your chosen representative of the Divine. You may recall the example of the *gopis*, who, although engaged in their daily mundane activities, were always thinking of Krishna. While cooking, cleaning, doing other household duties, walking or talking, the mind was always on Krishna. No matter what they were doing or where they were going, nothing could take their minds off their Beloved Krishna; they were in constant meditation on Krishna Consciousness.

Even the replay of any spiritual act is meditation. For instance, when you have been in the presence of your *Guru*, remembering His Wisdom, listening to His words and contemplating on His discourse, you can return to that event in your mind and you can visualize yourself sitting there, listening to His words and connecting with Him. That is meditation.

This kind of meditation is very easy because you have already participated in the event; you have gone through the experience. Now all you have to do is to replay it in your mind. Thus it becomes a spiritual activity. In that sense, any positive act, any experience, can become meditation. You can look at a flower and observe the color and the texture of the petals – or observe the details in the flame of a burning candle – this becomes meditation. There are so many possibilities for meditation, so many choices. The best way of course is to simply glide into meditation effortlessly, where everything just flows. It is like going to bed and just sliding off into sleep rather than making an "effort" to sleep. Struggling to go to sleep is an unpleasant state of mind: you end up tossing and turning with a determination to make yourself relaxed enough to go to sleep. This does not work. The more you try, the more restless you become. It is only when you give up the struggle that you can sleep.

Vedanta describes a state of being as *sahaj*, sliding into a totally calm state of consciousness without effort, like an ability to switch on and off. This can prove to be a useful ability when trying to tune out disturbing outside noise or distractions. You can compare this to the ocean. Although the ocean creates constant waves of movement, deep down in the ocean, everything is perfectly calm, despite all the activity of the waves that are created on the surface. Similarly, emotional waves are being created constantly, whereas deep inside you there is perfect calm and peace. This is your True Nature. Indeed, the practice of *Sahaj Vasta* is an effortless way of meditation – an innate sense of knowing that you are on the right Path and in the right state of mind, always calm and just observing, thereby tuning into your True Self.

Sometimes your spiritual journey can be very painful and yet your journey can also be very pleasant. What is it that determines whether your journey is painful or pleasant? It is the very idea of having to try so very hard which makes your journey unnecessarily difficult and painful. Try to start with the easy Path, the Path of the *gopis*. Their constant focus on

Krishna Consciousness had become a beautiful meditation, and eventually, after Krishna left, they became Enlightened.

Many people thought that the *gopis* were sad and mourning. There was Uddhava, devoted disciple and friend of Krishna, who suggested to Krishna that what the *gopis* really needed was Knowledge: "They have not learned from You yet, oh Krishna." Krishna said: "Alright, fine, it seems I have failed; maybe you can teach them." A delighted Uddhava, fully aware of his importance, set off towards Vrindaban to find and teach the *gopis*. The *gopis* were happy to receive the great friend of Krishna and eager to receive a message from their Beloved. Uddhava began to instruct them in *Vedanta* and the Path of *Yoga*. All the *gopis* listened courteously and with great attention to the long lecture. When the discourse ended one of the *gopis* stepped forward to ask a question: "Oh most learned friend of Krishna, we hear the teaching and knowledge you bring us, but tell us, oh Wise One: when every single cell in our bodies, each thought of the mind is filled with Krishna, with no space for anything else, where shall we put your knowledge?"

That statement was the Enlightening Knowledge for Uddhava. Although a truly learned man, he had not yet reached that height of the *gopis'* consciousness – and humbly he acknowledged the Illuminating Knowledge he had received from the *gopis*. Krishna represents the Totality and Supreme Consciousness: as the *gopis'* total beings merged with that Totality, there was no more duality. They had become Krishna themselves.

That message clicked with Uddhava and he realized that the *gopis* had reached the Supreme Height. While Uddhava was still using his mind, intellect and reasoning and crawling through truth, the *gopis* had become Truth. That was the lesson Krishna had wanted Uddhava to learn. Uddhava had considered himself the great teacher and *guru* and he had to discover that the *gopis* actually were the *Guru* and he, the learned Uddhava, was the student.

The point is that once you merge into the Totality, you no longer have a separate identity. There is no longer the small "i" – i, me and mine have vanished. The test is when you are still disturbed by small things that happen in life; if you get upset by comments made by others, there is still much to learn. The whole idea is to overcome fear, doubt and all the tricks of the ego. Ego is the most difficult aspect to handle. If you do not have devotion, dedication and love, ego can become a monster – and you become its victim.

It can happen that someone in very modest circumstances, by the Grace of the *Satguru*, is being given the opportunity to advance him/herself both materially and spiritually. Unfortunately when affluence has been achieved, the almighty ego often takes the credit, sometimes to the extent of looking down on those in more modest material circumstances. Did you forget that the good fortune is the result of Divine Grace alone, and that the purpose of the improvement of your circumstances was for further spiritual development? It is sad that just a little material success can get you so lost on the Path you once vowed to take.

That kind of arrogance is the work of ego and a totally distorted and imbalanced mind. The power of *Maya*, illusion, is extremely strong. *Maya* can come in different forms and different persons to test and to deceive you, to lure and to destroy you. It is good to remember that *Maya* can give generously – but she can also take away. It is not easy to overcome the workings of *Maya*.

A small anecdote on the methods of *Maya* is depicted in an episode of Narada, the Great Traveler and Vishnu's favored disciple. One day, Narada approached his *Guru* and informed Him that he had mastered *Maya* very well. Yes, indeed, he now had a real handle on *Maya's* workings. Vishnu listened smilingly and a little later He asked Narada to take his *lota*, his little pot for drawing water, to go to the river nearby and fetch some water. Narada went about his errand, but as he approached the river, a big wave washed over him and, losing consciousness, he was swept away.

When consciousness returned and he opened his eyes, he saw to his astonishment that he was surrounded by a large group of people observing him expectantly. Apparently the king of the country had died and the astrologers of the country had stated that that the first man seen would be the next king. That first man was Narada. Narada was taken to the palace where he was crowned and informed of his responsibilities. Very quickly he got to like this new life of wealth and power, with a beautiful queen at his side and he ruled the country in luxury and style for many years.

The years passed until one day a big plague descended upon his kingdom and many people died, including his wife and children. Narada the king was totally alone as he stood by the river, crying bitterly as he cremated his family.

Having completed this sad task, Narada decided to take a cleansing bath in the river and he submerged himself with all his emotional pain in the waves of the river. However, emerging from the water, he was surprised at the change of scenery. Nobody was around and nothing was there – just his little *lota* lying next to him. It was then that he remembered. He picked up his *lota* and took the water back to Vishnu who said: "Hmmm, you were gone a long time..."

The lesson is that *Maya* can give and also take away even more than you started off with. It is good to remember that nothing was ever "yours" to begin with. You cannot establish ownership over that which was not yours initially. Blessings and boons are being given to you for a very specific purpose. Whatever is given to you is not actually yours but to be used for a Higher Purpose. When you forget and claim it as your own – "it is mine, I have earned it, I worked for it" – that kind of forgetfulness reflects the illusion of *Maya* and it can have devastating effects.

In today's news we see the many exposés of human egos that have run rampant and we also see the consequences. Forgetting the illusion of *Maya* is a very difficult task; only when you surrender to the Highest in humility can *Maya* be managed – and you have to remind yourself, again and again. This happened to King Janaka, a very noble king. Everything was excellent in his kingdom and although he was a wise and enlightened person, there still remained some vestiges of "I" and "mine" in his mind. Eventually, when he found his Master he stated: "I will give my kingdom to you." That utterance was his mistake; for that one comment opened a whole lecture on what is "yours" – on ownership. That one comment led to so much Knowledge that later these discourses became known as *Ashtavakra Gita*.

Well, that is the way of a true Master, of the *Satguru*. You may make a statement and He will keep quiet, but if He takes your statement seriously, a whole discourse of Knowledge may emerge.

It is important that you examine what you say before you actually verbalize your thought. Often statements are made mechanically, whatever comes into the mind, without thinking and often without knowing what you are talking about. The serious implementation of mindfulness will help to overcome this habit through the practice of meditation.

17

The Benefits of Meditation

Some people ask: what is the advantage of doing meditation – what benefit do I gain from that practice? The first benefit of meditation is the calming of your mind, making it peaceful and balanced. The second benefit is a drastic reduction of stress. The third benefit is the balanced functioning of your whole physiological system: your blood pressure normalizes, your heart beat and your pulse become regular and calm, promoting effective circulation whereby all bodily functions stabilize.

Then what are the spiritual benefits? Clarity of thought, freedom from fears of the unknown and from insecurity, having confidence in yourself, an absence of worry and anxiety, and the removal of phobias – these are the internal, spiritual benefits. The most important of the spiritual benefits is the free flow of spiritual thought and spiritual Energy. Your mind is tuned to the Source where unending water flows, which means spiritual thought and inspirational Wisdom and Knowledge. While that is the highest potential, even the achievement of just some of these benefits will help your development tremendously. There is great value in this practice and you will see which benefit is coming to you.

It has been mentioned many times that the mind can be very muddy. Take the example of having to draw water from a tap and you see muddy water pouring out. You know that at some place, somehow, the water got polluted. Similarly, the mind can also become polluted. You may wake up in the morning with your mind all mixed up, perhaps as the result of some nightmares, perhaps you have a headache or feel anxious, or you are unwell and feel depressed or confused and you do not feel like doing anything at all. These examples are all parts of a "muddy" mind.

A clear mind on awakening is happy and looking forward to the new day. This is the time to attend to and solve any concerns, clearing any mundane matters. You may go about your daily activities with happiness all around you. Nothing has actually changed on the outside, but the clear mind has perceived everything in complete clarity.

For the muddy mind, the day may be wonderful and sunny outside, but if your mind is not clear, your whole perception will be different and cloudy. Sometimes you may not know why this happens, you cannot find the cause, but this is how body and mind work. All sorts of impressions are accumulated, whether negative and positive, happy and unhappy. These are manifestations of duality and they become part of your system. If the majority of elements are negative, the manifestation in body and mind will be equally negative. If the majority of elements are positive, there will be an equally positive reaction. That is why your practices should be positive.

Another question often raised concerns the subject of relaxation. Many people consider going on vacation for their relaxation. For instance, a trip to the seaside, lying on the beach or going to luxury destination may appeal to you. This may appear like relaxation, but in your mind you are already back at the workplace or in your home, already dealing with all the potential issues that may arise when you get back. That is not real relaxation, although it may appear so to you at the time. Real relaxation is when your mind is also calm and peaceful, not only the body.

Once I was giving a talk at a big conference when a politician approached and informed me that he was following my teachings; teachings I had given many years previously. This gentleman reminded me of my advice that wherever you are, at home, at the office or at a factory, concentrate on that job entirely and conversely, when at home, just focus and pay attention to your family. Do not mix home and work. He said that he had followed these instructions and was happy to report that it had worked out perfectly: the job was going well and his family was happy.

When you go on vacation with a muddy mind, it does not mean that you are relaxing, for that has to come from a mind which is free from worry and concern, not wondering who to call, where to go and what to buy. There are all sorts of outer forces governing you just waiting to trip you up. The point of concern is whether you allow this to happen. Outer forces – which are no fault of yours – will always be there trying to disturb you. If not in obvious form, these forces can sneak in subtly, barely noticeably, and if not recognized, they can create havoc in your life.

It is your spiritual *sadhana*, your practice, how you receive those forces and how you deal with them. How do you avoid a reaction in the face of abuse or accusations? However, if you can remember to think of it as a play, you will not react. It can also be that there is someone around you, maybe in your family, who constantly nags and complains. It is possible that after some time you have learned to tune out all the nagging and complaints and you no longer react.

The question is who is in control of your senses − is it you or the person who is "attacking" or trying to get a reaction from you? When you are in control of your senses you can dictate your own terms; whereas if you allow the other person to be in control, this can frequently make you unhappy. It is in your power to make the decision not to be disturbed by outside elements, no matter what. A relaxed mind will help to tune out outside disturbances.

Relaxation can be in many forms: for instance, a harmonious relationship can also be very relaxing, maybe listening to soothing music over a cup of tea, or going for a pleasant stroll in the countryside together while listening to the birds, watching the play of light and shadow, or listening to the wind in the trees − the examples are endless. Relaxation is a state of mind, not of your environment − although the right environment can be helpful. The important thing is to avoid negative surroundings whenever possible and seek a calm and pleasant environment.

That calm engendered by relaxation will help to lead you smoothly into meditation. It is that state also when all other sounds − like noisy machinery or a persistently yapping dog − disappear into the background. Everything vanishes into the background and you go beyond.

When you engage in all appropriate and beneficial spiritual practices − like meditation − gradually you become immune to unpleasant situations and you can move towards wholeness. That is the aim of your life.

18

A Guided Meditation

In silence you hear yourself, in silence you know, in silence you experience and in silence you perceive; therefore silence is the very part of yourself. In silence you integrate the Knowledge; in silence you discover the Ultimate. Silence speaks in silence.

Feel that all the senses are relaxed; every part of the body should be relaxed and comfortable; any negativities which may have come to the body are disappearing. Say to yourself: "I am not the body, I am not the senses, I am not the mind, I am not the soul and all the identities which have been imposed upon me − I am nothing − and yet I am everything."

By contemplating each thought, that I am not this, and I am not that, you become attuned to the Energy of your Life Force.

The very bliss which you hold lets you experience your own Light and your own song, thereby dissolving all the conditions of the mind which has created so many impressions throughout your time.

Feel that all these conditions are being dissolved.

Feel: "I am Total Consciousness, Pure Consciousness: I was never born, nor am I going to die, there is neither birth nor death."

All that appears so overwhelming in fact is passing, as with a moving cloud.

The reflection of yourself is everywhere: "I am reflected on each and everything the senses are dealing with."

Therefore you are not the participant; nor are you involved in the play of *Mayavik* or illusion. You are the main Source, the Ultimate Reality.

Experience that state of consciousness through meditation and contemplation. It will help you to achieve that state where nothing will affect either mind or body.

Since thought is very strong, and thought affects the senses, the senses will act and react accordingly. Once the thought is clear, there will be no reaction within the senses. Senses will behave according to the prevailing situation or circumstances.

When you no longer identify with the senses, sense object or with the thought, you will cease to experience suffering, because attunement to the Totality is always there: "I am the Totality; I am the Absolute and the Bliss. That is my Reality. That is what I am – all other things have been created around me. I have created many things that are not really a part of me, although they appear to be so."

Fear, for instance, can be created when you perceive a dangling rope to be a snake; yet once you realize that the rope is just a rope, fear will simply disappear. When you come to know that the potential threats you may perceive do not actually exist, there will no longer be pain, suffering or pleasure. Instead there will be the spontaneous bliss which has always been there.

The body is the vehicle in the dualistic state of

consciousness. In the non-dualistic state of consciousness, there is no body or mind. However, in the dualistic state, the body becomes your vehicle and that vehicle is intended to take you to the destination of Total Freedom or Liberation from which you are bound.

It is your own mind which creates a wall and there is no difference between the space outside the wall and within the wall's boundaries. It is only perceived as a confined space. Space is not confined, for when the wall is removed, you will realize that there is no difference between the space within and without.

Likewise, removal of darkness and removal of ignorance will create a different state of consciousness: the real state of consciousness where you will recognize your Totality. Thought is very strong and thought can dissolve ignorance – supported by the Knowledge of "Who I am" and "What I am."

The constant reminder of: "I am not this, I am not that" will take you to the place where you realize Who and What you really are.

Your thought has to be very strong and "burning" constantly, like a flame that is burning all the time, not letting darkness enter. That Knowledge has to be prevalent in the mind at all times so that the mind does not become clouded by impurities – so that the mind can perceive in clarity and in Light.

Therefore alertness is necessary and the application of the Knowledge of the Ultimate Reality. It is essential that from time to time you contemplate the question: "who am I? Am I the body, the mind, or the senses?" That contemplation will inspire the mind to maintain the standard of consciousness.

Having that Knowledge of the Source, the senses will no

longer be subject to action and reaction, knowing that the five elements of the body can only survive and exist by the reflection of your own energy. You are not the elements.

Once this thought process is controlled, there will be an absence of reaction within the mind and within the senses; there will be an absence of fear and of negativity as well as an absence of all those forces that are obstructing or confusing you like a prisoner and the real view of your Self.

Having achieved that, it is like going beyond the clouds where a very clear vision of space and Light is revealed. There is no space as such; knowing that space has no boundaries, space is infinite. When you know your own Infinity, there is no beginning and no end.

All those contemplations from time to time will inspire and help you to move further and further. Once that thought is clear, everything else will be transformed. There will be no reaction of any kind in that state of consciousness. Perception of everything is changed and you begin to see things very differently than before this change took place.

Therefore, the practice of contemplation, meditation and analysis from time to time is very important to maintain your own awareness of what is required for self-inquiry, Self-discovery. You are always the Source. Once the course is established there will be no confusion. Through Knowledge, you can inspire yourself and help yourself to experience the Truth.

There are many different ways to meditate. Meditation can also be done while walking, talking or working. While the mind is dealing with all the required actions for the particular tasks, there is also that aspect of mind which is tuned to the

Source. You may be doing all the external activities, yet you can experience the state of meditation and you will be unaffected.

Suffering of mind and body is of course a real thing, but suffering exists because the perception is one of attachment to places, persons or things, as well as to thought. All these attachments will create suffering. Therefore the state of non-attachment is recommended.

You either have everything or you have nothing; either everything belongs to you or nothing belongs to you; you are either in everything or you are in nothing. You are no longer confined in any particular situation; your consciousness has become expanded consciousness. You could call it a widening of your horizon, where you neither lose anything, nor do you gain.

Coming back to the *karmic*, dualistic state of mind, the unfoldment of *karma* will take place every now and then. Of course there is a stage when one goes beyond *karma*; but so long as you are bound by *karma*, *karma* will take care of the entire process of pain, suffering, pleasure, dying and being born again. This is the unending continuous process, irrespective of being in a body or not. The difference is that while you are aware of why things are taking place, there will be minimal reaction. In contrast, if you are subjected to a situation where your vision is clouded and you lack the panoramic or Cosmic View, you are caught in the situation, caught into the process of *karma*, and you identify with the suffering, pain and pleasure. It is again a point of identification: "I am this, this is happening to ME!" Ask yourself: "which I, which me, is the one affected?"

There is no I, ME and MINE. Instead think: "I have no form, no form as such, and if it appears that I have form, then it will soon be over. Therefore I cannot be my form, it cannot be my name, because as the body dissolves, so does my name. This name and this form to which I am so much attached and on which basis I communicate and recognize myself are completely unreal in the end. I know that I am not this and not that; what I am, you are too – and what you are, I am too."

Such contemplation will let you recognize other aspects in yourself without any conflict whatsoever, bringing harmony within yourself and letting the process take place. The *karmic* process of *Maya* – although *Maya* is an illusion – also appears to be real in daily life. At the same time, one who knows *Maya* and what appears to be real recognizes it as just an illusion. Complete recognition of One Self in its Totality is to be pursued and to be attained.

That is the meditation to be practiced.

19

Managing Relationships

A question which is often raised concerns relationships, especially within a spiritual community. Many feel that there are very few truly spiritual role models; moreover those few role models that emerge in the spiritual field often do not have many worldly possessions and do not appear to be very active in mundane matters. This prompts further questions, such as: "If I were to be serious about this Path, and I end up alone, with no money or possessions and all my sources of entertainment, will I miss out on all the good things in life without any relationship?"

I have already said that if you have desires, it is better not to renounce. Indeed, you can integrate or live in parallel by following the Path while engaging in the world. If a High Being decides to become a householder, He or She will be a perfect householder; a High Being will know exactly how to deal with all situations that may confront a householder. The only problem that could arise is that the other partner may not be able to cope with the Energy intensity and manifestation of such an advanced partner, unless they have also achieved some understanding. Actually there have been examples in the spiritual history when there have been perfect partners, husbands, even kings and other rulers who were Enlightened Beings.

The key point is that an Enlightened Being would have no difficulty in dealing with any problem in the world. Spiritual practice is not an escape from life. It is not that they become solitary because they cannot cope with daily problems; rather it is because they have gone through all tests that they have acquired all the skills to cope with anything life can present. They can deal with any type of life, whether political, professional, business or otherwise. Some High Beings also have been householders for a period in their lives. Svami Ramatirth for example: He invited His family to come with Him to the Himalayas and although they accompanied Him to Rishikesh, eventually they turned back, as they were not ready to cope. A Perfected Being also has no problem of being without money – it becomes irrelevant to their lives. Look at some of the great Avatars like Rama and Krishna: they too had partners and lived an exemplary life.

However, for those who have not attained the lofty heights but are striving towards that goal, a relationship is definitely not an obstacle and can in fact be helpful, provided that, as mentioned, the partners are in tune with each other and both are striving for the same goal. However, if the partners' expectations are different from each other, that could lead to disharmony on their respective paths. If there are different perceptions, different desires and expectations, there will be some difficulty. On the other hand, if the goals are fundamentally similar, there should be no problem in walking the Path together. The ancient *Vedic* concept of marriage in India was based on the principle of walking together towards Enlightenment. This concept would make the journey easier for many nowadays. Joining in marriage had Enlightenment as the objective.

When it transpires that at times one partner keeps moving on the spiritual Path and the other partner is far less inclined to do so, then the question arises: Is it appropriate for the spiritually focused partner to wait until the other person "catches up" or should he/she keep going? Remember that the final goal for every person is to attain Enlightenment. The great poet Saint Tulsidas answers the question very bluntly: "Those who do not support you in your endeavor to reach the final fulfillment – regard those as your direct enemies." This may sound very harsh at first, but spiritual fulfillment, communion and union with the Divine have to be the priority – it is the very purpose of life.

Therefore, if one partner is not quite ready to follow the spiritual Path, he or she can always continue later, whenever that individual is ready. In the event that one partner decides to sacrifice his/her momentum towards the final goal, then both partners would be stuck at the same level and the one who held back would be very unhappy, since the drive to continue towards fulfillment had been blocked. This conflict has to be resolved. It will not disappear until the Path to the final goal is resumed and concluded.

One who is in love only sees and hears the Beloved, and nothing else. One who is in love only experiences the Beloved. Nothing else can penetrate or disturb. Spiritual Knowledge is often described as "nectar." A time will come when the partner too will "thirst" for this Knowledge, and, just like having an unquenchable physical thirst, this thirst for Knowledge of the Ultimate Self - *Atma Bodh* – will persist as a constant longing for the Ultimate Knowledge.

Ask yourself: how can anyone taste that "nectar" once and not miss it thereafter? The mystic, Saint Mira, calls this an "addiction" which reaches far beyond one's physical life. Narada, the Great *Bhakta*, calls it a "Pursuit for Eternity" of that Divine Love, Divine Wisdom and Divine Knowledge. Anyone who has tasted this nectar once can never be satisfied and will always long for more. A person who has had that experience and has suspended the pursuit has never really understood this Mystery to begin with. If your spiritual pursuit stops somewhere, it means that you have not understood at all. Many people start following the Path and after some time, they drop off, or get side tracked or caught in something else. Then further development stops. Yet something intrigued them, and triggered their interest, but they did not understand the True Nature of Knowledge.

The pursuit of Knowledge is also the pursuit of happiness and bliss. This happiness and bliss is not only for a lifetime: it extends far beyond one lifetime. When you do not continue in this pursuit, you are actually denying your very Self. The Teachings that are being given to you are eternal and not just for a few people, but for millions of people for all the time to come. The effect is eternal. For all the seekers of the future who are longing for this Knowledge, this is the opportunity given to them.

On that basis, any kind of relationship, worldly or otherwise – whether with partner, family, children, business partners or others – all have to be resolved. This is the very nature of things. Unless all conflict, all issues have been resolved, settled and concluded and you have closed these chapters, they will come back to you. There is no escape.

One of the biggest hindrances on the Path towards fulfillment seems to be attachments – to people, places and things and especially to a partner in a love relationship. Many may feel that living without attachments may prevent them from being able to love fully; that they may become passive or withdrawn.

You need to know that attachment is derived from

selfishness; it is not a positive attitude. Being attached to someone does not mean that you are helping yourself or that other being. Rather try to evolve; that will help both the other person and yourself. Any and all attachments will bind you on the physical level. It also does not help others. Instead, it will bind you in continuing the cycle of attachment – the cycle of birth and death.

Detachment, in contrast, will not bind you. It does not mean that you do not care. This is often confused. Caring is essentially a different aspect of love. Attachment takes place on the lower level of consciousness, whereas on the higher level of consciousness there is no such thing as attachment. Instead it becomes a fulfillment of any kind of relationship.

Attachment can create obsession, anxiety and fear. Some disciples may become obsessed with the *Satguru*. If that obsession deals with the *Satguru's* Teaching, that is wonderful, but if obsessed with His physical form, that will not help you to advance. Actually, it may hold you back if you cannot get past the physical connection. Whereas attachment to His Knowledge and His Presence is a wonderful thing, if you feel that your claim on His Presence is yours alone, you are actually working against the Nature of the *Satguru*. His Nature is Universal and you cannot keep Him confined in the small cage of an obsessed mind. Becoming attached to the *Satguru's* Knowledge will result in a form of *bhakti* – in love and devotion. This kind of attachment will never bind – instead it becomes spiritual *sadhana* and it will uplift you and further your growth.

One thing is very clear: spiritual growth with its goal of Liberation has no time limit and no time factor. There is no way of telling how long it will take for any individual. It can happen tomorrow, this lifetime, next lifetime – it depends on many things:

on your wishes, your longing, your attitude, your sincerity and intensity of striving.

It may even happen that one day you wake up and everything appears changed; you see things in a different light; you view the world with a different eye – the Spiritual Eye. Your whole perception is changed and things no longer appear as they used to. Everything is transformed.

Some people may question their suitability or fitness for the attainment of Enlightenment because they may have done too many "bad things." But if they *truly* realize that they have done too many bad things, these bad things can disappear in the process of self-correction and spiritual striving, provided their regret is sincere.

The great mystic Saint Valmiki was a highway robber before He realized His wrongful ways. One day He met Narada, the great Cosmic Traveler – a meeting which forced the thief to look at and examine His wretched lifestyle. The experience was such a shock to the robber that He surrendered to Narada, asking for advice on how to change His life. After being initiated by Narada, followed by long and arduous *sadhana* and *tapasya*, Valmiki became an Enlightened Being and the first to write the epic *Ramayana*, the story of Lord Rama.

Valmiki's story illustrates that once you know your Self, you have every reason to overcome your limitation. The act of surrender is like going into a different dimension, a different way of your own understanding. It resembles evolving from body consciousness to a Higher Consciousness. Surrender is a method of overcoming your own duality and your own ego. The act of surrender itself is a great *sadhana*. You climb and move into a different dimension. Otherwise you can remain stuck on the level of body consciousness: "I am" – "I am the body, the doer, I am desire." Surrender is a great act of evolving into a different level of your own understanding. It involves sincerity, recognizing your True Self. Think of a small child who surrenders and is totally dependent on the parent, accepting whatever may come. In a way this will bring a kind of peace within the individual.

Remember the story of Draupadi who was in trouble when the demon was humiliating her by attempting to disrobe her, pulling off her *sari*. Even then, she still thought that she could help herself – manage the situation herself – maybe with the aid of one of her husbands. Only when that too failed did she realize that only Krishna could help in this desperate situation, and as she surrendered to Him she received His support and was rescued by the Divine Intervention. As long as you are holding on to your self-determination you are deprived of that Energy. Surrender will allow you to enter into a different dimension and Grace Energy.

The point is: when you know that you are doing everything possible in your *sadhana*, when you have done your act of surrender, your pursuit of *bhakti*, implementation of the Knowledge, you will also know and feel that you are protected.

20

Honesty on the Path

Question: When someone has a True Teacher, one is sure to be on the Path that eventually will bring you to the goal. Is it possible though that the disciple may delude him or herself to be following the True Path? How can we know that our striving is authentic and genuine and that it is not just the ego which tries to pretend? How can we avoid such a trap?

Svamiji: This is something which you should be able to know yourself. Compare this to your eating of spoiled food: you may then suffer from an upset stomach. You know you have eaten something bad – no one needs to tell you not to eat the same thing again. If you are free from being defensive and offensive, free from acting and reacting, you know that you are in the neutral zone and your consciousness is objective. Then you are aware of what is happening in your body and in your mind – what is happening with your inner Self. However, when in an emotional state, you can hardly be objective and the mind will justify every act.

You have five different kinds of prana as mentioned in the Patanjali *Sutras*:

- *Prana* - controls the physical breathing process. *Prana* takes energy in the form of oxygen.

- *Apana* - controls the excretory organs and the reproductive organs.

- **Samana** - assists in the process of digestion and controls hunger.

- **Vayana** - the upward-moving breath, which directs the flow of *prana* from the lower to the higher planes of consciousness.

- **Uдhana** - controls the vocal chords, helping in breathing air and eating food.

The main *prana* is being assisted by four sub-*pranas*. One *prana* – *apana* – assists the release of the toxins from the body and the main *prana* is connected with the heart. The sub-*pranas* support the other functions.

Similarly you also have five minds. *Vedic* tradition speaks of five kinds of mind, one main mind and four sub-minds:

- **Manome** - mind;

- **Praname** - understanding *prana*;

- **Aname** - concerns physical aspects and nourishment;

- **Jnaname** - relates to knowledge; and

- **Anaндame** - bliss.

Much depends on which mind you happen to be in. For instance, if you have done something – right or wrong – and when you are in a stable mood, then you know exactly how to evaluate your act, whether you have handled yourself correctly or not. Moreover, when you are on the Path you will usually develop the instinct of discrimination much more. Your intuition becomes much more powerful. However when less developed, your intuition and your instinct are clouded. As you evolve, those two forces become very powerful indeed and spontaneously you know what is what and where you stand. You will have insight and you will see your future far more clearly, even when meeting a person and intuiting whether that person is conducive company or not or whether an object is helpful to you or not. It is like a cleansing process.

How do you clean your soul, your consciousness? Indulging in Knowledge or in Spiritual Energy becomes a cleansing process. A meditator in traditional *Vedic* form will say: "I am cleaning my inner self (*antakaran*), my inner sanctum. I cannot possibly invite my Beloved since my inner sanctum is not clean." He will not expect the Divine to enter his consciousness unless he has cleaned his thoughts and his mind. There has to be a purification process that will clean your inner chamber to remove the layer of dirt, impurities and negativity that can be so thick, especially living in the prevailing society of the lowest consciousness.

For example, there was a man who had been very active in the old communist regime. He mentioned that only recently had he become aware of a healthier and happier outlook. Reflecting on his old lifestyle it was only now that he had become aware of living positively, eating the right food, having right thought – spiritual thought. Having spent half a lifetime drowning in alcohol, eating all kinds of *tamasic* and unhealthy food and living in an atmosphere of violence and deceit, then, at the age of fifty, he became determined to transform his life after the supposed "good life" of excess living. Only then did he realize that what was considered "high living" was actually poisoning him. For him it was a relief to discover a balanced way of thinking and living.

Similarly, there was a king who had renounced the world and penned his thoughts of transformation: "Oh what a fool I was – under the impression that I was enjoying life and I discovered that I was not the one who had enjoyed my desires and objects of desire and all the tempting things around me, rather I discovered that *it was I who was being enjoyed by them.* But now that I am awake, I realize that." There are people in this world who seem to have some evolved trait. To be at the height of material success and to be able to look at one's life with a spiritual focus indicates that there must have been some spiritual connection from the past. There are such people in the world who awake from a long slumber to long for spiritual nourishment.

Normally you think that you are enjoying various delights and entertainment until you find out that it was the other way around. Your enjoyment was nothing but an illusion. This illusion must be removed. *Vedantic* Knowledge reminds us that you do not have to renounce everything – it is all there for you, it is a gift. Only beware that you do not become the victim of any gift, that they do not use you and you do not use them. Rather, make good use of any gift in your life, whether it is your body or your mind or your senses. Find out how you can make the best use of such blessings that they may help you to grow towards your evolution.

This Path is not a fad or phase. If material wealth could make you happy then the wealthy would not be so unhappy. Consider: what is the richness in your life? You may not know that while you are a very fortunate being, you have only experienced poverty due to your own mindset and lack of self-responsibility. One can pretend to be a disciple of the Teacher and delude oneself. In order to progress one must follow the Teachings with constant sincerity and review: you have to be alert and watch.

Sometimes people will say that they want to please the Teacher. Well, the only real way to please the Teacher is to implement and follow His Teaching. That realization is not a whim of heart or mind, it is a True Realization of Who I am, What I am, and what I have to do to keep myself steady on the Path so I do not fall down, get side-tracked or get caught or blocked. This involves all other aspects of your role – *dharma* – that you have to play in this world. If your priority is the spiritual life, you must integrate your role in the world of *Maya* in accordance with your spiritual discipline. No matter what events take place, all this is part of your *dharma*.

One man had a dream: he met a woman and fell deeply in love – the love was mutual between both people. It was a very fulfilling relationship, lasting for many years, and the couple traveled to many places. Eventually the day came when the husband spoke to his partner that after all this wonderful time together, the purpose of their togetherness had been fulfilled and the time had come to part and for each to go his and her own way. At that point he awoke. He expressed his puzzlement that when he woke up he did not feel any pain, sorrow or regret whatsoever. Instead, he felt an immense fulfillment. He also felt that it had been a very real happening – although a so-called "dream," it did not have the dreamlike quality but instead he perceived it as a real experience.

An explanation was that what he had gone through in his dream was a very unique and wonderful event, an event beyond time and place. This kind of experience most people do not have in a lifetime. The amazing truth is that he had a sense of fulfillment. Such an experience is beyond human explanation. How is it possible that you can catch the essence of such beauty and fulfillment in such a short – apparently – span of time? All the events, all the places visited – the amount of experience he had in this dream – recalling all of this would normally take years. How fascinating it is that this, which was perceived as a dream, cannot just be regarded as a dream – but an experience in a different consciousness. Then what is this – is it time speeded up? Again the question of what is real arises: what is fulfillment, what is happiness?

Such kinds of experience are simply wonderful and very precious – very few humans are so fortunate as to have this kind of experience in their lifetime. In this example, this was especially fortunate since in his current lifetime he did not have any experience of love. In fact, the little moments of happiness people experience in life are just a taster to real true and wholesome contentment. Unfortunately, people often search in the wrong places and do not follow the True Search, thereby wasting an entire life.

Examining all aspects of yourself is very fascinating, whether this is your physical aspect, your emotional aspect, your psychical and spiritual aspects and finally your innermost Self. All are part of your Self and all have meaning and purpose. Experiencing any of these aspects, at times you may ask yourself whether this is real or not. Sometimes you may be relaxing and dozing and maybe at that moment you have some astounding reflection. Most people have experienced this. Where is this kind of signal coming from and why is it being sent? That is why life is so mysterious as well as mystical. Life is a puzzle that has to be solved.

The *Satguru* can guide and explain through the Teachings to put things into the right perspective. But one has to remember that the waves on the water are not created by the water but by the wind. Any fluctuation of mind, any conflict or crisis, is not you. Some gust of wind has sprung up and created the waves in your mind – just let this pass. Only once you let it pass, then comes the peaceful calm and you will feel refreshed and clear. Remind yourself that all these things are being created within and around you as a *sadhana*.

In nature, when they have problems, many animals isolate themselves to recuperate until they recover. They go through the healing process without noise or broadcast. It is unfortunate that humans often seem to feel the need to let others know about their pain and propagate a crisis rather than modify it. It is much more important to let the healing process take place. That is something people have to learn, for when you are in extreme pain, be that a physical pain, mental anguish or emotional pain, there comes a detachment and that can be a very powerful element. If you are attuned to the Teachings, this can also bring greater Knowledge and acceptance.

Many have been practicing various methods of spiritual practice and gone through all kinds of tests and that has brought some fruit: now they should prepare for the greater fruit. Make use of the Knowledge and the Teachings all the time. There is evidence all around you to teach you, and when you have discovered that, you begin to appreciate everything that comes. When attuned to your *Satguru* and His Grace, Knowledge and Grace Energy, then you are protected, you are inspired. Thereby you have opened the channel for further energy and development within yourself.

One should always be filled with ongoing happiness. Moments of despair may occur from time to time: this is the time to be honest with oneself, remember the Teachings and to attune to – and remind oneself – of the words of Wisdom and Truth spoken or written.

Glossary of Key Terms

Sanskrit Terms

Adharma   That which is not in accord with the divinely given law of nature; an unwell or unnatural state of imbalance

Adhyatmik   Pertaining to the Self, individual and Supreme

Ahimsa   Non-violence, non-injury in thought, word and deed (see *yamas*)

Anand(a)   Bliss or pure happiness

Anahata   Lit: unbeaten, unstruck; *Anahata* (heart chakra). *Chakra* name of the 4th mystic circle or energy wheel along the spine in the region of the heart

Antakaran   The inner sanctum of yourself

Artha   Resources or wealth

Arjuna   Receiver of Knowledge in the Bhagavad Gita; friend and disciple of Krishna who reveals the sacred knowledge while on the battlefield of Kurukshetra (field of the Kurus).

Asana   Lit: sitting down- yogic body posture. Posture; seat; hatha yoga postures; discipline of the body to keep it disease-free and for preserving vital energy; the third limb of Patanjali's Eightfold Path

Ashram/asrama   Training school for spiritual aspirants – center for learning and growing under guidance of bona fide *Guru* and spiritual retreat

Atma(n)   The Self, the Immortal Soul

Aum   Sacred mystical syllable beginning, middle and end; highest spiritual sound and vibration; the first sound of creation: AUM, representing the three gods: A – Vishnu, U – Shiva, M-Brahma; preservation, dissolution and creation respectively; essence of the *Vedas*, the *pranavas*

Avatar   A divine incarnation

Avidya   Ignorance; absence of Knowledge or wisdom

Bhagavad Gita   "The Divine Song" - a celebrated mystical poem of 18 chapters, containing the sacred dialogue between Krisna and Arjuna. Krisna's teaching to Arjuna in the form of a mystical poem. A major spiritual and philosophical treatise; the key source book of Hindu philosophy

Bhajan   Devotional song

Bhakti   Transformed and universal spiritual love and devotion

Bhakti Yoga   The path of loving devotion to God – of selfless dedication to the Highest

Brahma   "The Creator" one of the Hindu trinity that is Brahma the Creator; Vis(h)nu, Preserver of virtue or goodness and Siva the Destroyer of all negativity

Brahman	The Supreme, Absolute and Ultimate Reality, the eternal all-pervading, all knowing, changeless Consciousness; God – the Divine Essence, Imperishable Great Principle, Universal Soul
Brahmacharya	First 25 years of the life - devoted to studying and building the body and mind
Buddha	Siddhārtha Gautama, Divine Incarnation – teacher of Spiritual Truths and historical founder of Buddhism – 5th Century BC.
Chaitanya	Awareness; One who is spiritually aware
Chakra(s)	Energy center in the form of a wheel situated in the subtle body
Chit (Chitta)	Consciousness; subtle energy; substance of the mind; Seat of bliss; also "longed for"
Darshan	Lit: vision, view; meeting with a spiritual purpose; sight or presence of the *Guru*.
Dharma	Law; duty; right conduct; righteousness, good works
Dhyana	Steadfast meditation; unbroken state of thought flow; the seventh limb of Patanjali's Eightfold Path
Dvaraka	From *dvar* meaning "door" – the door to Krishna Consciousness or Krishna *Loka*; the Divine Abode and Kingdom of Lord Krishna

Gopis	Milkmaids of Vrindaban and great devotees of Krishna
Grihstha	Second 25 years of life – devoted to accompanying duties and responsibilities of householder
Gunas	Lit: string or thread – as an abstraction it refers to 'tendencies', to the three subtle qualities, the fundamental operating principles or predispositions of *prakriti*, the universal nature. Each being is subject to these tools of *Maya*, the great illusion. Creation could not have taken place without these three subtle qualities, influences or moods:

- ***Sattva*** - the quality of light and positivity;
- ***Rajas*** – the driving force for passion and activity; and
- ***Tamas*** – the signature of darkness, inertia and negativity.

Guru	*Gu* – darkness; *ru* – light; the preceptor or spiritual guide who takes you from the darkness of spiritual doubt into the Light of Knowledge - *"Guru Granth Sahib"* – Sacred Book of the Sikh Religion – regarded as the last *Guru*
Hatha Yoga	Union of positive and negative energies; physical exercises which promote the balancing of positive and negative energies within the body - (see asana); also: withdrawing the mind from externals
Ishv(w)ar (Isvara)	Lit: the most capable, Supreme Being; God
Janaka (King)	King of Mithila – enlightened ruler

Jiva	Living being
Japa	Repetition of certain sacred syllables
Jnan(a)	Higher Knowledge – Knowledge which sets you free from the bondage of the world
Kabir	14th century mystic poet of India revered by Hindus, Sikhs and Moslems alike; gave a new direction to Indian philosophy Example: "Like the seed contains the oil and the fire is in the flint stone, thus your temple seats the Divine. Realize this if you can."
Kali	Mother of the Universe in Her time-annihilating aspect as the Goddess of Destruction; the Black Goddess; consort of Shiva; the divine Mother in her destructive and cataclysmic aspect
Kali Yuga	The Dark Age, the last of the Four Ages, Age of negativity and destruction
Kama	Fulfillment of positive ambitions and desires
Karma	1. Action, work, deeds, performance; 2. the result or effect of one's actions
Karma (Karmic) Law	Law of cause and effect or compensation
Karma Yoga	The yoga of selfless action or good deeds – not seeking recognition or reward for one's actions
Koshas	Five aspects of the self or "sheaths"; one of five coverings of the *Atman* or Self according

to *Vedantic* philosophy

Krisna (Krishna)	Divine Incarnation of *Vishnu* – Stories and teachings associated with Him represent an integral part of Hindu philosophy with applications for daily living
Kriya Yoga	Gross and subtle techniques and practices to break the limiting conditioning of body and mind
Kundalini	"The Coiled One" – serpent power at the base of the human spine – Divine creative energy latent in the human being
Lakshmi	Consort of *Vis(h)nu*; Goddess of wealth and beauty
Lila	Divine Play; Divine Love actively engaged in worldly affairs
Mahabharata	The Great War – famous epic in verse, narrating the battle of the Bharatas
Mandala	Circle, disc, orb
Mantra(m)	Concentrated energy of certain sacred sound syllables
Maya	The great illusion of the world as reality and worldly objects; Mother Nature
Mithila	Ancient Indian country in Northeast India – birthplace of many Enlightened Beings
Mira	16th century Rajput princess, daughter of King Ratan Singh; mystic saint who was intoxicated

with Divine Love for Her Lord Krishna

Moksha Liberation or Enlightenment

Mudra Hand postures or gestures in yoga that are used to balance the elements in the body and direct the life force in specific healing directions

Narada Also known as Narada Muni with his *vina*, is a Divine Sage and ardent devotee of Lord Vishnu, often referred to as the cosmic traveler with the ability to visit distant worlds or planets.

Niyama Observance; second limb of Patanjali's Eightfold-Path:

- **Shaucha** – purity, cleanliness;
- **Santosha** – contentment, peacefulness;
- **Tapas** – austerity, spiritual discipline;
- **Swadhyaya** – spiritual self-study; and
- **Ishwarpranidhana** – offering one's life to God

Paramahansa Lit: Supreme Swan, a person of the highest spiritual realization, being reflecting swanlike qualities such as discrimination; one who sees himself as what he or she is

Parasmani A substance able to turn base metals into gold; also sometimes claimed to give immortality

Patanjali Ancient logician and grammarian; author of the *Yoga Sutras*, the first systematic compilation of *yogic* science

Prakriti Primal cause, creative force, Nature (female principle)

Pran(a)	Vital Life Force, also Breath of Life
Pranayama	Control of vital life force (normally through breathing techniques); the fourth limb of Patanjali's Eightfold Path
Prasad	A gracious gift offered to a deity and then distributed to followers with the deity's blessing
Pratyahara	Withdrawal of senses from their external objects; balancing of the senses; the fifth limb of Patanjali's Eightfold Path
Puja	Expressions of honor, devotion and worship
Purna	Meaning Whole; derived from root *"Pri,"* meaning to fill; full or complete; infinity, totality, entirety and completeness
Purusha	Supreme Being, Universal Soul – animating principle in all beings (male principle)
Ramayana	Famous epic in verse narrating the life of Rama, seventh complete incarnation of the Godhead
Rajas(ic)	One of the three *gunas* – subtle quality of passion and activity – associated with the color red
Rajram	Kingdom of Lord Ram in the Golden Age
Ravan	Demon king of Lanka, said to have ten heads (ten outstanding qualities)
Sadhana	Spiritual practice for the purpose of upliftment, of overcoming one's human limitations, ascetic

– one who has dedicated his life to spiritual pursuit

Sadhu Seeker of truth – travelling mendicant, ascetic – one who has dedicated his life to spiritual pursuit

Samadhi Lit: joining; union; ultimate accomplishment; highest consciousness; ultimate state of consciousness; Wholeness of Self; the eighth and final limb of Patanjali's Eightfold Path

Samskaras Latent, ingrained tendencies of the personality

Sankalpa Desires, wishes, resolves, intentions with determination, commitments

Sanskrit Most ancient, totally logical language – still in active use; root of present Indo Aryan languages

Sanyasa Last 25 years of life – devoted totally to spiritual development

Sat Truth, existence, reality

Satguru Highest, Supreme Teacher; True Master who takes the seeker from darkness to Light

Satsang Sat – truth, sanga – company; lit: "higher association with Truth;" Keeping the company of Saints, Enlightened Beings and their Teachings

Sattva/Sattvic One of the three *gunas* – subtle quality of light and positivity – associated with the color white

Seva	Selfless service without expectation of recognition or reward
Shakti	Power, energy, the Divine Power of Cosmic Energy
Shiva	Personification of God as Destroyer – third in the Hindu Trinity
Svami (Swami)	Lord, Master
Tamas(ic)	One of the three *gunas* – subtle quality of darkness, decay and negativity associated with the color black
Tantra/Tantric	Lit: stretching, expanding, spreading; scientific doctrine of affirmative approach relating to the power circuits within the human body; a path to liberation, to expand consciousness and to liberate energy
Tapasya	Lit: to burn it; produced by heat; crucible of fire for purification; steadfast disciplines austerities and penances, the fire of which destroys impurities in the mind
Tirth	A place where a High Being has disseminated the Teachings; where the Divine *lila* has been played
Tulsidas	Gosvāmī Tulsīdās (1532-1623) Indian poet and philosopher saint – considered one of the greatest and most famous of Indian poets. He is regarded as an incarnation of Valmiki, author of the epic *Ramayana* written in *Sanskrit*
Upanishads	Essence of the *Vedas* – dialogues of

philosophical and spiritual wisdom

Vanaprastha	Third 25 years of life devoted to semi-retirement and dedication to more scholarly and social work

Vedanta   "Complete knowledge of the *Vedas*" – the Ultimate Truth as testimony of the great books of wisdom: the *Brahma Sutras*, the *Upanishads* and *Bhagavad Gita*. The System of Knowledge based on the essence of the *Vedas*, concerning the nature and relationships of 3 principles:

1. the Ultimate Principle;
2. the world; and
3. the individual soul

Vedas/Vedic   Lit: True or Sacred Knowledge; science, ancient, sacred texts of civilization, consisting of:

- ***Rigveda*** – dealing with true knowledge;
- ***Samveda*** – devotional and ritual songs;
- ***Yayurveda*** – dealing with aspects of health and medicine; and
- ***Atharvaveda*** – dealing with the aspects of Nature

Visnu (Vishnu)   Personification of God as preserver and sustainer of goodness and virtue – the Omnipotent, the Omniscient, the Omnipresent – middle One of the Hindu Trinity (usually the aspect that incarnates into human form)

Viveka   Discrimination on the basis of foregone investigation, resulting in true knowledge. Faculty of differentiating according to real lasting values; truth from untruth, reality from illusion

Yama   Self-restraint; the first limb of Patanjali's Eightfold-Path:

- **Ahimsa** – non-violence, non-injury: harmlessness;
- **Satya** – truthfulness, honesty;
- **Asteya** – non-stealing, honesty;
- **Brahmacharya** – continence; and
- **Aparigraha** – non-envy, non-greed, non-selfishness

Yoga   Lit: union; derived from the root YUK, meaning "to join" also translates as "yoke" impulses and inclinations of the ever wavering mind are brought under the discriminating yoke of the Higher Self; different types of yoga start with a different aspect and lead towards harmony and integration of the whole being

Yuga   Age, era, astronomical cycle of years; there are four *yugas*:

1. **Satya** – age of Truth; Golden Age;
2. **Treta** – age of triads; silver age;
3. **Dvapara** – age of twilight; and
4. **Kali** – age of negativity, darkness and machinery